KENNETH ERVIN YOUNG
ANGEL INVESTORS TO VENTURE CAPITAL

10-SLIDES TO STARTUP FUNDING SUCCESS

AN ENTREPRENEURS GUIDE TO STARTUP FUNDRAISING

BOOKS BY

KENNETH ERVIN YOUNG

ANGEL INVESTORS TO VENTURE CAPITAL — 10-SLIDES TO STARTUP FUNDING SUCCESS — AN ENTREPRENEURS GUIDE TO STARTUP FUNDRAISING

ANGEL INVESTORS TO VENTURE CAPITAL — INVESTOR DUE DILIGENCE — WHAT INVESTORS NEED TO KNOW TO FUND YOUR STARTUP — AN ENTREPRENEURS GUIDE TO STARTUP FUNDRAISING

Figure 1-Testimonials

If you need to raise money for your Startup, whether, from Friends and Family, Angel Investors, or Venture Capitalists, this is the one book you must read!

−−Thankful Startup Guy

I am at my 3rd try at starting a company, and I struggled the first three times to get funding. With this book, I was able to raise money in less than 30 days after my first pitch to investors.

−−3rd Time Startup Entrepreneur

After reading Angel Investors to Venture Capital − 10 Slides to Startup Funding Success, I finally understood what I was doing wrong after having not raised monies after six months of pitching to investors. Now I know what startup investors need to know when I pitch and how to put together the perfect 10-slide investor pitch deck. Many thanks!

−−I was Blind, and Now I can See Entrepreneur

ANGEL INVESTORS TO VENTURE CAPITAL
10 SLIDES TO STARTUP FUNDING SUCCESS

I had emailed my 30+ page Investor Pitch Deck to over twenty startup investors and was never getting a return email, and they would not take my phone calls. After reading this book I know I was going about raising money the wrong way and with the wrong investor pitch deck. I am re-writing my Investment Opportunity Story and creating a new Investor Pitch Deck after the model in the book, and I am confident of a better outcome as I move forward.

    ––1st Time Startup Entrepreneur

Why has no one authored a book like Angel Investors to Venture Capital – 10 Slides to Startup Funding Success before now? Kenneth has written the perfect How-To-Guide for both the first-time and tenth-time Entrepreneur on raising monies from anyone from Friends and Family through seasoned Venture Capitalists. This is the book to follow if you need to raise money for your Startup!

    ––Excited Seasoned Entrepreneur

I have been investing in high-technology startups for over ten years and am constantly frustrated by the inexperience I see from Entrepreneurs when they do their Investor Pitch to me. I am going to demand every Entrepreneur who wants to pitch read and follow Angel Investors to Venture Capital – 10 Slides to Startup Funding Success before I allow them to make an appointment for a First-Date Investor Pitch.

    ––Seasoned Startup Investor

ANGEL INVESTORS TO VENTURE CAPITAL

---

10 SLIDES TO STARTUP FUNDING SUCCESS

AN ENTREPRENEURS GUIDE TO STARTUP FUNDRAISING

Kenneth Ervin Young
Serial Entrepreneur & Business Coach
www.IdeaToGrowth.com

ANGEL INVESTORS TO VENTURE CAPITAL
10 SLIDES TO STARTUP FUNDING SUCCESS
COPYRIGHTS

Idea To Growth LLC

3690 W Gandy Blvd, Suite #183

Tampa, FL 33611-3300

Ken@IdeaToGrowth.com

Proof Reader: Kyle Edward Young

Printed in the United States of America. First Edition: 2019

Library of Congress Cataloging-in-Publication Data (applied for)

ISBN: 978-1-7198-2859-8: (Paperback Edition)

DEDICATION

Figure 2 - Dedication

For my two grandfathers, Carl King, and Jack Young. Both taught me much about fishing, respect for everyone around me and the value of honest work.

For my two grandmothers, Ida King, and Hallie Young. One who taught me how to cook and work as a team. One who showed me the power of education and crossword puzzles.

To my Uncle and Aunt, Bill, and Gladys Young. Thank you for your lifelong guidance and love.

For my Dad who taught me multiplication and division with blocks at an early age and put up with my teenage years.

For my Mom who taught me how to share and helped me deliver newspapers on my paper route when I was a teenager.

ANGEL INVESTORS TO VENTURE CAPITAL
10 SLIDES TO STARTUP FUNDING SUCCESS

To my wife, Sharon Prinsen-Young, who has both supported my lifelong entrepreneurial spirit and loved me for 30+ years, you help me laugh at life a little every day.

To my 24-year-old son who has overcome many challenges and is in college to earn dual AS Degrees, one in Computer Programming and the second in Web Development, all while employed part-time for Target and part-time for me as a Website Developer. He also was my primary proof reader for this book.

To L.J. Sevin, founder & CEO of Mostek Corp. and my first post-college Mentor. Although you have passed on to whatever greater beyond which waits for each of us, I still think of you often and how your USD 7.5mm first investment round, belief in our Cypress Semiconductor team and your mentorship, enabled the team to succeed and take Cypress to an IPO. Thank you!

To my Mentors who saw in me traits I may not have seen in myself and shared great guidance, you taught me much. I can never repay you for all your mentor help.

I am honored and blessed to have all of you in my life!

FAMOUS QUOTES

Figure 3 - Famous Quotes

If both your brain and body ache at days end, it has been a productive entrepreneurial day.

— Kenneth Ervin Young

When everything seems to be against you, remember the airplane takes off against the wind, not with the wind.

— Henry Ford

Only two things are infinite, the universe and human stupidity, and I am not sure about the universe.

— Albert Einstein

A business which only makes money is a poor business.

— Henry Ford

The definition of insanity is repeating the same action and expecting a different result.

ANGEL INVESTORS TO VENTURE CAPITAL
10 SLIDES TO STARTUP FUNDING SUCCESS

— Albert Einstein

It is strange only extraordinary men find the discoveries, which later appear so easy and straightforward.

— Georg C. Lichtenberg

If you think you can do or think you cannot do, you are (100%) right.

— Henry Ford

Attitude is a little thing which can be a significant difference.

Winston Churchill

   The journey of a thousand miles begins with one step.

— Lao Tzu

Science without religion is lame, religion without science is blind.

— Albert Einstein

The good thing about science is science is true whether you believe in science or not.

— Neil deGrasse Tyson

Success is not final; failure is not fatal: the courage to continue is what counts.

— Winston Churchill

Figure 4 - Note from the Author

This book has been read and edited many times in its construction to provide proper spelling, punctuation, and grammar, as well as accurate content.

However, like most events in life, goofs get by our best efforts. In the electronic publishing age today, it is quick and easy to correct all types of mistakes.

Please email me below any issues found. I will review and strive to correct any errors and update all electronic and future printings of this book.

Readers, I thank you in advance for your efforts to help me build this book as correct as possible.

Kenneth Ervin Young

Ken@IdeaToGrowth.com

THIS PAGE INTENTIONALLY LEFT BLANK

TABLE OF CONTENTS

ANGEL INVESTORS TO VENTURE CAPITAL
10 SLIDES TO STARTUP FUNDING SUCCESS

ACKNOWLEDGMENTS

Figure 5 - Acknowledgments

I want to acknowledge those who have pushed me for many years to share this information in book form, so my authorship could reach a broader audience. This book is proof persistence does pay off!

I want to acknowledge the many mentors I have been fortunate to find. Thank you for tolerance with my endless questions and your advice even when I pushed back or appeared to ignore your guidance. All those words rolled around in my head and bit by bit influenced who I became. Thank you.

To my many teachers from K-12 and college — thank you for your patience with a boy who sometimes misbehaved and sometimes drew outside the lines. I know now all my teachers always knew what I was up to even when I thought I had hidden my actions from you. My exploration of the many paths leads to both mistakes and successes from which I learned.

ANGEL INVESTORS TO VENTURE CAPITAL
10 SLIDES TO STARTUP FUNDING SUCCESS

To my Georgia Institute of Technology (GA Tech) fellow graduates who at graduation toss their caps up in the air and yell **We Survived** — Remember the moment for the rest of your life. Perseverance in a hard-earned degree shows in all one does in life. Dogged determination serves better than any other single skill learned at GA Tech.

To my extended Friends and Family who helped me become who I am today - Thank you. Each person had an impact on my life beyond what one might think. The best legacy we can leave behind is our influence on those touched.

DISCLAIMER

Figure 6 - Disclaimer

This book is available in Paperback, Kindle, Audible and PDF formats to reach the widest audience.

However, when the reader is ready to construct PowerPoint Slides, Google Slides or Apple Keynote Slides, I recommend one to read the book on an RGB color screen to best view the slide examples.

I urge my readers to first read the book on any platform of choice. When ready to create an Investor Pitch Deck use PowerPoint or another slide construction tool, open the book on an RGB Color platform to get the most from my lessons.

We took precautions to verify the accuracy of the information in the book, but the author and publisher assume no responsibility for any errors or omissions. The author and publisher assume no liability for damages which result from the use of the content within or for any other materials this book relates to within.

ANGEL INVESTORS TO VENTURE CAPITAL
10 SLIDES TO STARTUP FUNDING SUCCESS

Who Should Buy This Book?

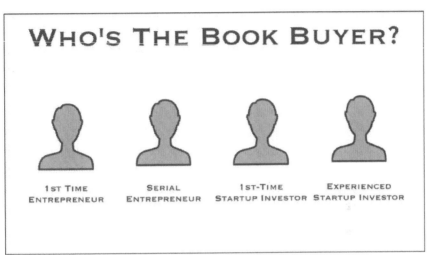

Figure 7 - Who Should Buy This Book?

Who should buy this book? You have asked a great question!

First-time Entrepreneurs

Most buyers of this book I expect will be entrepreneurs who want to start their first business and do so the best way possible.

My goal is to have every entrepreneur read this book and follow most of what they find within its covers. If each entrepreneur does follow my books teachings, a high percentage of high-quality teams and ideas will get in front of startup investors and have successful First-Dates. More successful First-Dates will lead to more successful companies. Everybody wins!

However, there is another group I want to represent 50% of my book buyers.

First-time or Infrequent Startup Investors

First-time or infrequent startup investors are those who desire the livelihood of a startup investor.

Why should first-time and infrequent startup investors buy my book?

First, by reading this book as a first-time or infrequent startup investor, you will learn what questions a startup investor should ask and the answers a startup investor should expect to those questions from an entrepreneur before you invest.

Most of us have heard the saying **You do not know what you do not know**. Our inexperience in any subject means we never know all the questions we should ask. My book will help the entrepreneur and startup investor acquire greater knowledge and have fewer miss-steps.

Second, as a first-time or infrequent startup investor, I want your first investment to have a higher likelihood of a positive experience and financial outcome. I want the startup investor to have a higher level of confidence when they invest money into a startup and team.

Many startup investors waste both their time and the time of the entrepreneur with multiple meetings, but the startup investor never pulls-the-trigger and invests in the startup. Many reasons exist for this outcome. One reason is the startup investor lacks the confidence in their knowledge to make a wise investment. My book intends to help instill the confidence a startup investor wants to feel when they make a startup investment.

PREFACE

Third, I believe part of the job of every startup investor is to help their startup teams. Most startup founders will not have read this book. Once a startup investor has read my book, within the first five minutes of your First-Date with an entrepreneur, you will realize the entrepreneur needs to read my book before they meet with you again. I want the startup investor to send the entrepreneur to my website, the bookstore, the Amazon website, or any of my other book outlets, and tell the entrepreneur to buy this book. Once the entrepreneur has read and implemented my teachings, the startup investor can have the entrepreneur reschedule for a First-Date do-over. This First-Date do-over will be a more meaningful experience for both the startup investor and the entrepreneur, with the increased likelihood of a Second-Date invitation as the outcome.

Experienced Startup Investors

Why should an experienced startup investor buy my book?

To save the experienced startup investors most valuable asset — time.

As an experienced angel investor or venture capitalist, your most valuable asset is your time. Many experienced startup investors employ interns or junior staff to read the deluge of Investor Pitch Decks they receive weekly. Most Investor Pitch Decks lack the critical content a qualified startup investor needs for a successful First-Date (first meeting) with an entrepreneur.

How can the experienced startup investor use this book to save your valuable time?

ANGEL INVESTORS TO VENTURE CAPITAL
10 SLIDES TO STARTUP FUNDING SUCCESS

First, the experienced startup investor can have your junior staff share a link to this book with any entrepreneur whose idea may fit your investment profile.

Second, the experienced startup investor can post a link to this book in the FAQ section of your website and encourage entrepreneurs to read and follow the teachings of my book before a First-Date with a startup investor. Every entrepreneur I have ever met would kill to know a technique to improve their odds to get a First-Date with a startup investor.

Third, the experienced startup investor will have fewer unqualified entrepreneurial First-Dates. Some entrepreneurs will self-select out of a First-Date with a startup investor after an attempt to implement the methods I teach in this book. The Investor Pitch Deck construction techniques I teach in the book will help entrepreneurs realize their idea has too small of a market for most startup investors. Other solopreneurs will learn from the book they may need to build a core management team before a First-Date with some startup investors.

The bottom line is both new and experienced startup investors can use my book to help get better-qualified entrepreneurs for a First-Date.

Serial (Repeat) Entrepreneurs

So why should serial (Repeat) entrepreneurs buy this book?

First, just like startup investors, time is the serial entrepreneurs most valuable asset. Do not waste a First-Date by lacking information startup investors want to see in the Investor Pitch Deck. If the Investor

PREFACE

Pitch Deck misses critical startup investor information, you have wasted the time of at least two people.

Second, like first-time or infrequent startup investors, most serial entrepreneurs do not know what they do not know. This book will educate the serial entrepreneur, so they appear as a seasoned entrepreneur to a startup investor. Most startup investors do not want to hold the hand of the startup entrepreneurs in which they invest. This book will help the serial entrepreneur become more experienced and need less startup investor hand-holding.

Third, and this is for the serial entrepreneur, we can all learn how to handle challenges and events better the next time around. The first few times I was involved in a startup, I did not possess the wisdom I have shared with you in this book. My Investor Pitch Decks and oral presentations were horrendous. Our teams still got investment capital, but in hindsight, it was painful. In a few cases, startup investors pulled me to the side after my presentation to offer guidance. These startup investors told me what information as the entrepreneur I needed to remove and what other information I needed to include in the Investor Pitch Deck to better address their questions.

Their startup investor guidance was eye-opening. Before the investor guidance, I built Investor Pitch Decks with no idea what a startup investor wanted to learn. When startup investors told me what they wanted to learn about the startup and I followed their guidance, the startup investor pitch First-Date led to frequent Second-Dates.

ANGEL INVESTORS TO VENTURE CAPITAL
10 SLIDES TO STARTUP FUNDING SUCCESS

Remember, an invite to a Second-Date with the startup investor is the goal of the entrepreneurs First-Date with a startup investor.

Also, be sure to check out the Resources page for helpful downloads! There is also a link to save you dozens of hours building your own Investor Pitch Deck Slide template. For book buyers I include a discount code that will save you $$$.

Click RESOURCES to jump to the download page now.

PREFACE

Chapter Quiz

Q1: Should any person interested in becoming an Entrepreneur buy and read this book? [YES] [NO]

Q2: Should a person doing a startup for the 2nd or 3rd time buy and read this book? [YES] [NO]

Q3: Should a first time Angel Investor buy and read this book? [YES] [NO]

Q4: Should a "seasoned" Angel Investor buy and read this book? [YES] [NO]

Q5: Should a Friend or Family Member considering investing in a startup buy and read this book? [YES] [NO]

Q6: Should a first time Venture Capitalist buy and read this book? [YES] [NO]

Q7: Should a "seasoned" Venture Capitalist buy and read this book? [YES] [NO]

Q8: Should any person working in a High Technology Accelerator or Incubator buy and read this book? {YES] [NO]

BONUS: Should every person who has read this book and gotten value from it recommend this book to other Entrepreneurs and Investors they know? [YES]

Answers:

https://ideatogrowth.com/answers-10-slides-to-startup-funding-success/#preface

Chapter Notes

Fundraising — The Investor Needs Come First

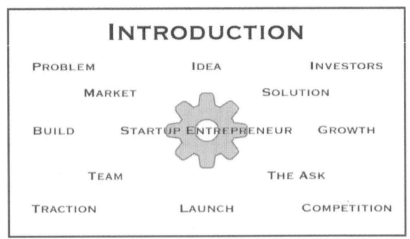

Figure 8 - The Entrepreneur & The Startup Investor

As part of my Business Coach role, I mentor entrepreneurs who run startup to multi-million dollar businesses. Some of these startup executives are members of the Tampa Bay WaVE, the local Tampa Florida High-Technology Accelerator. The Tampa Bay WaVE started in 2008 as a meetup group for high-technology startups in the Tampa Bay area by Linda Olson. She and the other members found terrific value in meeting on a regular basis to discuss startup challenges and seek advice on solutions. After a few years, the meetup group formalized as a non-profit company. In 2014 millions of dollars of funds came in the form of a grant. With these funds, www.TampaBayWave.org was off to the races. Now some 100+ companies (mid-2018) are active members and have to fundraise more than USD 100M of Other People's Money (OPM).

ANGEL INVESTORS TO VENTURE CAPITAL
10 SLIDES TO STARTUP FUNDING SUCCESS

The teams I was privileged to be part of throughout my career have had several successful exits. In total, these startups received more than USD 100M in venture capital. In my last venture-backed startup, my team and I fund-raised more than USD 87M through our first three Silicon Valley venture capital funding rounds (Funding Round Series A, B & C). I learned a lot from experiences on how to fundraise. But, I learned more from the various mentors who were kind enough to help me along my journey.

When you need Other People's Money (OPM) to grow your startup, one of the essentials entrepreneurs will need to create is a startup Investor Pitch Deck. How to develop and use the startup Investor Pitch Deck to get OPM is why I authored this book. My experiences with my own companies and my work with angel investors and venture capital firms for more than 25 years, I have learned many Do and Do Not items about how to fundraise. In this book, I will share with you what I have learned. You will learn what startup investors seek in a team and garner an idea of why a startup investor invests. The entrepreneur will also learn items which will kill the investment opportunity for the current startup, and for any future startup, they may start.

In my business coach role, I have reviewed many Investor Pitch Decks used to startup pitch to everyone from Friends and Family, to angel investors and up through venture capitalists. I have seen five-page Investor Pitch Decks. I have seen 100+ page Investor Pitch

INTRODUCTION

Decks. I listened to the types of questions startup investors ask. Over time, I began to realize something important.

It is All About What the Investor Wants to Hear, Not About the Startup Story the Entrepreneur Wants to Tell!

Allow me to explain. When you go to a bank to get a loan for a home or car, what is the primary goal of the banker?

To get 100% of any loans back, plus interest.

Guess what. The startup investor has the same goal.

How does the banker accomplish their goal?

By diligent choice of borrowers with an acceptable level of risk.

Guess what. The startup investor has the same plan.

How does the banker minimize risk?

By proper choice of borrowers with a good credit history, good income, and signs of stability.

Guess what. The startup investor seeks the same characteristics.

Unique and sometimes hard to measure traits exist for a startup investor to seek in an entrepreneur before investing. Below are a few of the critical items.

HONESTY — Above all else, any startup investor wants to work with honest people. How does a startup investor measure honesty? Over time. The startup investor will inject questions to test the entrepreneur's trustworthiness. I coach there are three words/phrases an entrepreneur should say in response to most questions.

- Yes.

- No.

- I am unsure of the correct answer, so let me investigate, and I will get back to you.

Often the startup investors question needs a simple Yes or No. When a startup investor hears a long-winded answer without a clear Yes or No response, one instinctive reaction is the startup investor believes the entrepreneur's responses are B.S. A long-winded answer can infer to a startup investor the entrepreneur is dishonest. Big red flag.

INTEGRITY — This is a close cousin of Honesty. Integrity is a measure of your moral values. Do you treat all of those around you with respect? Do you joke about how you cheat on your taxes? Do you brag about how you have gotten to where you are in life and business solely on your own accord? These characteristics are often a sign of how successful, or not the entrepreneur will be in their attempt to attract and assemble a formidable team.

COACHABILITY — Coachability is the ability to listen and learn from others. I have coaching applicants who in a matter of minutes, I determine are uncoachable. How? I discover a person is uncoachable through some natural observations. Uncoachable candidates talk too much and ask few questions. Uncoachable candidates repeatedly interrupt. Uncoachable candidates state or infer the answer to the question is wrong, or the startup investors statement is incorrect. Uncoachable candidates tell me someone else screwed up a project the entrepreneur oversaw, and none of the failures were the fault of the entrepreneur. Uncoachable candidates ignore startup investors questions and respond tangentially.

A Balance of REALISTIC and OPTIMISTIC — In the construction of the Investor Pitch Deck, the entrepreneur must do a lot of business research. Part of this research involves how long it takes and to what size the entrepreneur can grow sales. Of course, the entrepreneur makes an educated guess. But the sales forecast should be an educated guess. By educated guess, I mean you learn the size of the Total Available Market (TAM). The entrepreneur breaks the market down and shows which parts the market the startup will be the Serviceable Addressable Market (SAM). The entrepreneur has researched and understood the competition, the market segment, and the customers. Analysis of the startup core strengths versus the competitor's core strengths is critical. To know how the startup will get traction and the costs in time and investment capital is vital. Has the entrepreneur created worst-case and best-case sales growth scenarios? Will the entrepreneur share a plan which weighs success and risks with believable balance? This Balance is how many startup investors measure how realistic versus optimistic the entrepreneur is.

When an entrepreneur puts together an Investor Pitch Deck, they gather a lot of information. Sadly, the entrepreneur often constructs a 20, 30, even as much as 80+ page startup Investor Pitch Deck.

Most humans have a short attention span. Even advertising networks know most ads longer than 30 seconds are too long for most consumers. For startup investors, the successful length of an Investor

Pitch Deck is about ten pages and three to ten minutes in total oral presentation length.

This book covers the ideal content, order, and flow of the Investor Pitch Deck. By the end of this book, the Reader will have learned how to craft the startup Story into a successful ten-page Investor Pitch Deck. The Investor Pitch Deck, along with a great idea and team can help the startup fundraise.

In the next chapter, I will speak about — the 4 Stages of Successful Business.

INTRODUCTION

Chapter Quiz

Q1: The Investor Pitch is:

[ ] All about what the Entrepreneur want to say to the investor.

[ ] All about what the Investor wants to learn about the Company

Q2: 4 key things an investor is looking for in an Entrepreneur.

Q3: What is TAM short for?

Q4: What is SAM short for?

Q5: What is the typical attention span of a human watching an ad?

[ ] 30s [ ] 45s [ ] 60s [ ] 90s [ ] >90s

Q6: An investor wants an Entrepreneur to be wildly optimistic. [ ] True [ ] False

Q7: Answering an Investor question with a "Yes", "No" or "Let me look into that and get back to you" is always wrong. [ ] True [ ] False

Q8: The Entrepreneur should always interrupt the Investor to stay on schedule. [ ] True [ ] False

Q9: Sometimes telling little white lies to an investor is OK. [ ] True [ ] False

Q10: Telling an investor that you are responsible for all of the company success to date in your multi-person startup is OK. [ ] True [ ] False

Answers:

https://ideatogrowth.com/answers-10-slides-to-startup-funding-success/#introduction

Chapter Notes

Why the Business Lifecycle is Key to Funding Success

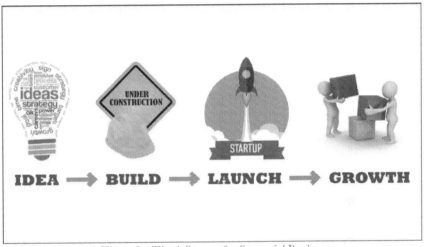

Figure 9 - The 4 Stages of a Successful Business

As a business coach, I work with companies at all four stages of the successful business life-cycle. These stages many refer to as:

- the IDEA Stage,

- the BUILD Stage,

- the LAUNCH Stage, and

- the GROWTH Stage.

These four stages of successful business life-cycles are what inspired my current startup name - IDEA TO GROWTH LLC.

Each of these lifecycle stages has a specific purpose. For the successful fundraising, every entrepreneur must understand the successful business life-cycle stages, and at which life-cycle stage the startup exists.

How do I define each of these four successful business life-cycle stages?

The IDEA Stage

The IDEA Stage is the first stage of a successful business. The IDEA Stage often begins when an individual chooses to stop **working for the man** and chooses to start **working for themselves**. The IDEA Stage is when an individual has an *aha* moment, which often occurs when the entrepreneur faces a problem, and none of the solutions that exist are good choices.

The IDEA Stage is what I refer to as the big homework business stage. While in the IDEA Stage, the entrepreneur should do the most sizable chunk of the homework on the IDEA.

Sadly, many Startups skip the necessary homework during the IDEA Stage, and the result is the startup wastes months if they jump too early into the second stage of a business, the BUILD Stage.

When the entrepreneur skips crucial IDEA Stage homework, the sad result is often the startup closes months or years later when there is a discovery of a critical piece of information. The entrepreneur has also spent both personal funds and often Other People's Money (OPM) too early.

But, the most critical item the entrepreneur has wasted is Other People's Trust & Goodwill which is all but impossible to get back.

What are some of the homework the entrepreneur needs to do to complete the IDEA Stage of the startup successfully?

THE 4 STAGES OF A SUCCESSFUL BUSINESS

Below are some of the critical homework items the entrepreneur should complete while in the IDEA Stage before they jump to the BUILD Stage.

- Record who the current solutions providers are
- Document who the customers are
- Record the price for each solution
- Document the leadership rank of each solution provider against the competition
- Record the overall world and regional market size in dollars and units
- Report the rough cost to manufacture and cost of sales for each competitor
- Record if the market is flat, in growth or contraction and by how much per year, forecast for the next five years
- Document if there are patents licenses needed
- Record critical product features
- Document estimated product costs to manufacture

There are too many IDEA Stage checklist items to list in this book, lest the book exceed a reasonable number of pages. However, I will provide you, as my reader, a link to a **100% FREE** Startup Business Life-Cycle Checklist. Below is the link:

https://www.ideatogrowth.com/contact-free-download-startup-business-life-cycle-checklist/

You can also find this link titled RESOURCES chapter at the end of this book, along with links to many other 100% FREE downloads from my website. Take a moment and check the link now.

Click RESOURCES to jump to the chapter now.

The IDEA Stage is where the entrepreneur analyzes the required management, other staff, and contract resources. I suggest every startup needs the critical management team members hired by the end of the IDEA Stage. The three essential management positions are:

- CEO - Who will Lead the team?
- CTO - Who will Design & Build the Product?
- CRO - Who will Sell the Products and Services?

Usually, the first entrepreneur of a startup is the CEO, at least initially. If the CEO of the startup has either a sales background or a technical background, this person may also serve as the CTO or CRO while in the IDEA Stage.

However, the CEO must choose which position is more important to themselves, and best served in, for the success of the startup company, while in the BUILD, LAUNCH and GROWTH stages. Each of these three management positions is a full-time job, and no person can do two jobs well. Identification of the replacement for the other job role should begin once the CEO chooses which job role to serve in long-term.

As an angel investor, one and two-person startups are more risky investments compared to three plus person startups. To get an investment from me, and from many other angel investors, each of the three critical management positions must have named persons who are ready to come onboard part-time or full-time before the startup investor invests.

Many startup investors have learned if an entrepreneur is unable to attract a management team, then the entrepreneur will often not be a successful CEO. As an entrepreneur, you should see this as the first test as a startup leader. This first test will be one of many tests to come.

The BUILD Stage

The BUILD Stage is the second stage of a successful business. The BUILD Stage should begin after the startup team has completed all the critical homework items while in the IDEA Stage.

The BUILD Stage is when the startup team builds the Minimum Viable Product or MVP for shorthand.

If the startup product is a durable good, now is the time to construct multiple prototypes until alpha and beta customers say *Yes, this is the product I will buy.*

If the startup product is a consumable good or Software-as-a-Service (SaaS) product, now is the time to go through the process of the construction of multiple websites or mobile application prototypes until the alpha and beta customers say *Yes, this is the product I will buy.*

In addition to the core three-person management team, the entrepreneur should name, by the end of the IDEA Stage, other staff members and contractors you will hire while in the BUILD Stage. These positions should all be outsourced positions while in the BUILD Stage. These positions are:

- Bookkeeper (outsource)
- Legal (outsource)
- Marketing (outsource)
- Website Development & Hosting (outsource)

The BUILD Stage takes time and capital. If the entrepreneur has assembled the core three-person management team as recommended, and the outsourced positions above, you now have additional essential tasks to complete. I list a few of these next.

- Find a lawyer experienced in working with startups.
- Form the startup (C-Corp or LLC) (use lawyer)
- Create founders and stock agreements (use lawyer)
- Create the customer-facing website
- Get required business insurance
- Create the MVP (Minimum Viable Product)
- Create the Sales Plan
- Create the Marketing Plan
- Get signed sales contracts from the first customers (I suggest the first ten). However, your startup may need more, or less, dependent on the market. What is crucial is the startup has enough sales to prove to the entrepreneur and startup investors customers will buy the MVP versus a competitive solution.

- Have the accounting package and website (if a SaaS business) able to accept payments from customers
- Have all the sales contracts written and blessed by legal
- Have all by-month budgets created and reviewed
- Assemble the Advisory Board and hold the first meeting

There are too many BUILD Stage checklist items to list in this book, lest the book exceed a reasonable number of pages. However, I will provide you, as my reader, a link to a **100% FREE** Startup Business Life-Cycle Checklist. Below is the link:

https://www.ideatogrowth.com/contact-free-download-startup-business-life-cycle-checklist/

You can also find this link in the Resources chapter at the end of this book, along with links to many other 100% FREE downloads from my website. Take a moment and check the link now.

Click RESOURCES to jump to the chapter now.

Advisory Board

An Advisory Board is a critical part of every BUILD Stage. Sadly, many startup teams either never assemble an Advisory Board, or construct an Advisory Board much later while in the LAUNCH Stage.

An Advisory Board created while in the BUILD Stage serves many helpful functions.

First, the Advisory Board is the startup teams sounding board. An Advisory Board listens to the management plans and challenges the startup will face as they execute on those plans.

Second, the Advisory Board can cover for management team positions which the startup team has insufficient financial resources to hire while in the BUILD Stage.

What skill sets does the entrepreneur need on a great Advisory Board?

- A person with a Marketing background who can help guide and assess the outsourced Marketing plan.

- A person with a Finance background who can help guide and evaluate the Budgeting plan.

- A person with a Legal background who can help guide and review all the Legal documents supplied by the outsourced legal firm.

- A person with a Sales background who can help guide and be a sounding board for the VP of Sales and the Sales plan.

- A person with a Technical background who can help guide and be a sounding board for the VP of Product Development and the MVP.

- A person with a CEO background who can help guide and be a sounding board for the CEO. The first-time CEO with a seasoned CEO on the Advisory board to act as a mentor always creates startup investor comfort. The existence of an experienced Advisory Board CEO means an easier fundraise.

These are the crucial Advisory Board members I urge the entrepreneur to find and assemble onto the Advisory Board.

THE 4 STAGES OF A SUCCESSFUL BUSINESS

While in the BUILD Stage, a process referred to as a PIVOT might need to occur. A PIVOT is a business term used by a startup to signal a meaningful change in the direction of the business.

A startup PIVOT might be a change from a Business-to-Consumer (B2C) business to a Business-to-Business (B2B) business.

A startup PIVOT might be a change from the sale of the product under the startup brand to the purchase of the product as a white-label product under the brand of another company.

If the startup does need to PIVOT, the BUILD Stage is the stage in which to pivot. If the startup waits until the LAUNCH Stage, or even worse, the GROWTH Stage, a pivot is costlier and may be fatal for the startup or the startup management team.

Many startups fundraise while in the BUILD Stage. However, to fundraise while in the BUILD Stage is a lot harder and will consume more time than at the LAUNCH Stage. An investment this early in the life-cycle of a startup is also a significant distraction to the startup team. An attempt to fundraise will delay the completion of the BUILD Stage checklist.

The startup CEO should assume they startup team will lose half or more of the team bandwidth to a BUILD Stage fundraiser.

The exception to this time-sucking fact is when the BUILD Stage startup does a fundraiser from one of the following sources.

- Friends and Family
- An angel investor in which there is already a relationship

ANGEL INVESTORS TO VENTURE CAPITAL
10 SLIDES TO STARTUP FUNDING SUCCESS

Friends and Family typically invest in the entrepreneur more than in the startup. It is rare for Friends and Family startup investors to have an extensive list of questions and documents like the typical angel investor would have. If Friends and Family are OK with the potential loss of 100% of their investment, then they can be an easy and quick source of BUILD Stage funds.

If the startup team has come out of an incubator or accelerator, a related angel investor may be comfortable with a BUILD Stage investment. Angel investors may also be suitable to seek a fundraiser from while the startup team still assembles all the Due Diligence expected by later-stage startup investors. What is Due Diligence? I will speak more on Due Diligence in the LAUNCH Stage section of this chapter and later chapters.

As entrepreneurs, you have a lot of work to do while in the BUILD Stage. If you must fundraise while in the BUILD Stage to keep the doors open, then you must do what you must do.

Remember also fundraising while in the BUILD Stage will cost the startup team more of the startup ownership. A higher risk exists for startup investors at the BUILD Stage than at the LAUNCH or GROWTH Stage. The higher risks startup investors take result in their demand for more substantial ownership of the startup.

When the entrepreneur has completed the critical BUILD Stage tasks, they are ready to transition to the LAUNCH Stage.

The LAUNCH Stage

The LAUNCH Stage is the third stage of a successful business. The startup has assembled the core management team. The team has built the Minimu Viable Product (MVP). The startup team may work towards a revision 2.0 of the MVP or even a second product. The startup team has all the fundamental business documents and processes in place.

In simple words, the startup team has completed all the critical tasks of a successful BUILD Stage and is ready to transition to the business LAUNCH Stage.

The LAUNCH Stage is all about the start of the ramp-up of the startup. The startup starts the ramp-up of the Product Manufacture. The management team begins to ramp-up with more team members. The sales team begins to ramp-up sales. The marketing team starts to ramp-up the Marketing.

Usually, the profit from the product revenue while in the BUILD Stage limits the startup growth.

The LAUNCH Stage is when most startups find there is a need for fundraising. The LAUNCH Stage is one of the simpler and lower stock dilution periods to fundraise.

By the start of the LAUNCH Stage, the startup team has done a ton of high-demand work and should have assembled all the Due Diligence startup investors need to see before a fundraiser. The startup is on a stable course, and startup investors can be convinced to invest.

I have mentioned the startup investor Due Diligence phrase again. What is the startup investor Due Diligence?

In the section after I speak to the GROWTH Stage, I will discuss the startup investor Due Diligence topic a bit more.

What are the critical accomplishments for a successful LAUNCH Stage?

- Secure enough funds to meet product sales demand
- The CEO, CTO CRO should all be full-time employees with the completion of enough investment to employ them.
- As sales ramp, start part-time and full-time staff for the positions below.
- Customer Service
- Marketing
- Shipping & Receiving
- Product Development
- Accounting
- Sales

The month-to-month budget plan should reflect the investment needed to support each business function.

Hire when needed and hire part-time until there is a full-time need.

The LAUNCH Stage is where the startup team will prove the product is or is not a high-demand product.

The LAUNCH Stage is also where the startup team proves whether the startup is one someone will want to buy for tens of millions of dollars (or much more) or if the startup is merely a lifestyle business.

A lifestyle business is one in which the operators earn a nice income, but the startup has insufficient sales and growth rates for most startup investors.

The GROWTH Stage

The GROWTH Stage is the fourth stage of a successful business. People ask me: ***When have I completed the LAUNCH Stage and entered the GROWTH Stage?***

No single benchmark exists. Many will use a financial reference.

One person might say when the startup has reached USD 1M ARR (Annual Recurring Revenue) or USD 1M in total annual sales.

Another person might say USD 10M ARR or USD 10M in total annual sales.

I propose a more straightforward benchmark.

When the startup can go to a commercial bank and get the funds needed to grow the startup at a high growth rate, without the need to co-sign the loan by the startup team, the startup has reached the Growth Stage.

The ability to borrow funds from a commercial bank means the startup has the choice to skip startup investor fund-raises yet continue to grow the startup.

However, a commercial bank loan could be a wrong choice for fundraising.

If the startup invests 100% of the profits back into the growth of the business, and the growth is still cash-strapped, the entrepreneur should use startup investor funds to build the startup.

Bank loans need payments each month that rob the startup of growth capital.

Uber and Lyft are two perfect examples of a startup investor-fueled GROWTH Stage fundraiser. While these two companies may take some bank loans for strategic reasons, those bank loans would have to be under favorable repayment terms. Loans secured with startup stock the bank could sell if necessary is standard. Dilution of the founders and current shareholders at an increased valuation is the preferred method to support sales growth while in the GROWTH Stage.

The GROWTH Stage is the most straightforward business stage to get startup investor funds and at the lowest stock dilution.

The GROWTH Stage of the startup never has to end if the startup team continues to execute well.

The GROWTH Stage has a path to a startup investor exit. The startup will have a financial exit when acquired by another company or when the startup has an Initial Public Offering (IPO).

The GROWTH Stage is the time while in which the management team should be open to acquisition talks. An acquisition as the startup ramps to more substantial revenue rates of USD 10M to USD 50M (depends on the industry) is common.

The GROWTH Stage is when the startup team, the employees, and the startup investors reap the hard-earned rewards!

Investor Due Diligence

Investor Due Diligence is the process startup investors go through when the startup investor chooses investable companies.

Investor Due Diligence is a combination of documents, interviews, and research startup investors and venture capital firms perform with each startup considered for investment.

Investor Due Diligence is a process which the entrepreneur should be prepared for before they do the first startup investor pitch.

Investor Due Diligence education is too much to cover in this book. The Due Diligence process is so detailed that I have a book, a course, and a SaaS product which I sell separately.

If you would like to get on my reservation list for my startup investor Due Diligence Book, Coaching Course and Software-as-a-Service (SaaS) product, click the link below to grab a spot on my reservation list. I will support a limited number of startups on both the Due Diligence Coaching Course and SaaS Product, and my book buyers get a jump to the front of my early adopter list.

https://www.ideatogrowth.com/contact-book-waitlist-investor-due-diligence-book/

ANGEL INVESTORS TO VENTURE CAPITAL
10 SLIDES TO STARTUP FUNDING SUCCESS

No credit card needed. All I need is your name and email. As soon as the Book, Coaching and SaaS product is ready for purchase, you will get the first emails ahead of my other followers.

In the next chapter, I will speak about whether the entrepreneur needs to use — Other-People's-Money (OPM).

Also, be sure to check out the Resources page for helpful downloads! There is also a link to save you dozens of hours building your own Investor Pitch Deck Slide template. For book buyers I include a discount code that will save you $$$.

Click RESOURCES to jump to the download page now.

Chapter Quiz

Q1: The 1st Stage of every successful business is the:
[ ] IDEA [ ] BUILD [ ] LAUNCH [ ] GROWTH

Q2: The 2nd Stage of every successful business is the:
[ ] IDEA [ ] BUILD [ ] LAUNCH [ ] GROWTH

Q3: The 3rd Stage of every successful business is the:
[ ] IDEA [ ] BUILD [ ] LAUNCH [ ] GROWTH

Q4: The 4th Stage of every successful business is the:
[ ] IDEA [ ] BUILD [ ] LAUNCH [ ] GROWTH

Q5: What is the earliest stage you should approach an investor?
[ ] IDEA [ ] BUILD [ ] LAUNCH [ ] GROWTH

Q6: What is MRR short for?

Q7: What is ARR short for?

Q8: You shouldn't assemble an Advisory Board until the Growth Stage? [ ] True [ ] False

Q9: What does it mean for a company to "pivot" and what is the best stage for a company to "pivot"?

Q10: What is "MVP" short for and in what stage should you have your first MVP?

Q11: The ability to get a bank loan signifies that what business stage?

Answers:

https://www.ideatogrowth.com/Answers-10-Slides-to-Startup-Funding-Success/#4-Stages

Chapter Notes

_____

_____

_____

_____

_____

_____

_____

_____

_____

_____

_____

_____

_____

_____

_____

_____

_____

_____

Is Other People's Money Needed for Success?

Figure 10 - Other People's Money (OPM)

As a Business Coach, I work with companies in all four stages of the successful business life-cycle.

These four stages of a successful business life I discussed at length in the earlier chapter are what inspired my startup name - IDEA TO GROWTH LLC.

Often when I first engage as a business coach with a startup, the topic of investment is an early discussion point. However, sometimes investment discussions never arise. Many startup teams first decision is not to use Other People's Money - OPM - to build the startup.

Why do entrepreneurs choose not to use OPM?

The first reason an entrepreneur may choose not to use OPM is the type of business itself. For example, you can set up a startup in which you sell the products or services of others.

How does one start this type of business?

Step 1: Find a distributor of low-end electronic products.

Step 2: Create a website where you list those products and find buyers to use these distribution products.

Step 3: Sell the items and collect the payments.

Step 4: Send the orders from the site to the distributor for order fulfillment.

Step 5: Pay the distributor.

The startup charged the customer when the customer placed the order then paid after the distributor shipped. The startup avoided the need to sell part of itself or to borrow money to create and build the business.

The second reason an entrepreneur may choose not to use OPM is entrepreneurs often start the business with savings and personal lines of credit. Entrepreneurs grow the business at a slow rate, with most or all the profits put back into the operation to sustain the business growth. Entrepreneurs know growth can be faster with OPM, but the startup does not qualify for business loans, or the entrepreneur does not the risks and headaches associated with a bank loan if they are eligible.

OTHER PEOPLE'S MONEY

The third reason an entrepreneur may choose not to use OPM is the desire to keep 100% ownership and control of the business. Entrepreneurs who strive to maintain 100% control of the startup can find this to be the right decision, but sometimes the avoidance of the use of OPM is an unwise decision. Below is one example in which the startup team strives to maintain 100% ownership of the startup is a rash decision.

John has started his business and grown the business to a nice size. However, if John had more cash to expand, John could increase the size of the business 500% in the next 12 months instead of the 20% he can grow the startup with the profits each month.

Now is the right time for John entrepreneur to use OPM.

Why?

Who would not want to grow sales 500% versus 20%?

When should John sell part of the startup, so the startup can grow faster and become more valuable?

John has managed to grow his startup to USD 1M/year in revenue at a 20% profit margin. Some of Johns clients have approached him, and these clients want to increase orders by 10 to 20 times the current order rate. Combined these order increases would grow the startup to USD 5M/year in sales in the next twelve months.

John finds a startup investor willing to invest in return for 20% of the startup. John accepts. Twelve months go by, and John increases sales to the expected USD 5M. John now owns 80% of the startup which did USD 5M in annual sales or USD 4M of the sales. The startup investor owns 20% of the startup or USD 1M of the sales. At a typical 3X valuation multiple on sales, Johns ownership is worth USD 12M, and the startup investors ownership is worth USD 3M.

What would happen if John chose against the use of OPM and instead chose to grow the startup by 20% using only the free cash flow from the startup profits? Over the same 12 months, the sales would go from USD 1M to USD 1.2M. John owns 100% of the startup. The same 3X valuation multiple on sales means the startup is worth USD 3.6M.

Should John want to be worth USD 12M and own 80% of the startup or USD 3.6M and own 100% of the startup?

The entrepreneur should be able to do the math for themselves (and the finance person should review) before the decision to take or not take OPM. Choose carefully.

I recommend startups delay the use of OPM funds until they achieve specific milestones. These recommended milestones are:

- Have built an MVP (Minimum Viable Product).
- Have many customers (exclusive of Friends and Family)
- Assemble the critical management team (CEO, CTO, CRO).
- Have the essential corporate documents completed and reviewed by a lawyer experienced in working with startups
- Have the accounting software in place

- Have the startup formation and stock documents created by a lawyer experienced in startups

The attempt to fundraise, other than from Friends and Family, before the entrepreneur has these critical milestones completed is a long-shot at best. I no longer invest in any startup until they achieve these milestones. Entrepreneurs will get a better valuation of the startup once they accomplish these milestones. Remember, the higher the perceived risk to the startup investor, the more ownership of the startup most startup investors will need in return for the higher risk.

The first startup in which I was a co-founder was in semiconductors (computer chips). The team had no choice except to use OPM. A semiconductor startup like the team started takes many tens of millions to tens of billions of dollars to create. Few individuals could fund such a startup themselves.

My first semiconductor startup took a Series A investment round of USD 7.5M (1982 dollars), and the investment lasted 12 months. The team got more than USD 30M (1983 dollars) in OPM in the Series B investment round. By the time we went to an IPO (Initial Public Offering) in June 1986 more than 80% of the ownership (and control) was in the hands of the startup investors. However, the team took the startup public 3-1/2 years after its start and made many millionaires in the process.

Bottom line. Put a lot of thought into the decision as to both whether and when to use OPM. This decision will affect the entrepreneur and the startup team for the life of the startup.

To aid you in the decision in when the best time for you is to take OPM, I have made a 100% FREE OPM Checklist you can download from my website link I share next.

https://www.ideatogrowth.com/contact-free-download-opm-checklist/

You can also find this link in the Resources chapter at the end of this book, along with links to many other 100% FREE downloads from my website. Take a moment and check out the link now.

Jump to the RESOURCES chapter now.

In the next chapter, I will speak about the Best Practices for constructing the Investor Pitch Deck.

Chapter Quiz

Q1: What is "OPM" short for?

Q2: Is it more likely a good or unwise decision to sell 20% of your company if the investment allows you to double revenue and profit in 12 months? [ ] Never! [ ] Maybe [ ] Good!

Q3: Do companies always need other people's money to grow and be successful? [ ] No [ ] Yes

Q4: You should always take other people's money even if you don't need it. [ ] Yes [ ] No [ ] Sometimes

Q5: Name three reasons an Entrepreneur may choose to NOT use OPM.

Q6: Capital intensive startups can always get to an MVP without outside capital. [ ] True [ ] False]

Answers:

https://www.ideatogrowth.com/Answers-10-Slides-to-Startup-Funding-Success/#opm

Chapter Notes

_____

_____

_____

_____

_____

_____

_____

_____

_____

_____

_____

_____

_____

_____

_____

_____

Do and Do Not's for Success

Figure 11 - Pitch Deck Construction Best Practices

Best Practices for Investor Pitch Deck

Before I get into the specific content creation details of each slide, I wish to start with my set of Best Practices the entrepreneur should follow to create the Investor Pitch Deck. Understanding the best practice guidelines will save you countless hours of edit time later. These best practice guidelines apply to every slide in the Pitch Deck and to the startup pitch presentation itself.

Ready? Time to learn my set of Best Practices to use throughout the Investor Pitch Deck.

Best Practice #1: Write the startup Story First

Why do I say, Write the Pitch Startup Story BEFORE You Create the Investor Pitch Deck? The startup Story is what the startup investor wants to hear about from the entrepreneur. The startup investor has no interest in a startup investor pitch deck full of pretty images, words, and numbers but lacking an excellent startup Story.

How does the entrepreneur start to write the Pitch startup Story? Start with the creation of a note, MS Word, Google Docs or similar file and name it Startup Name Pitch. Startup Name is the name of the startup.

Next, create ten pages each with one of the titles I show next.

1. Cover

2. Problem

3. Market

4. Solution

5. Traction

6. Competition

7. Monetization

8. Financials

9. Team

10. Ask

The startup CEO will present these ten slides in this order.

Why?

The startup CEO will author and present the startup Story in the order shown above because this is the order in which the startup investor wants to hear the startup Story.

Assume each slide has no more than three crucial points you will discuss. Some slides will have less than three critical points, but no slide should cover more than three vital points.

Why?

Google *The Rule of Three*. Many studies have shown the typical human brain can often remember words, numbers, and images with ease in groups of three. Take your social security number. The format is XXX-XX-XXXX. The dashes turn the Social Security number into a Group of Three. Therefore, a Social Security number is a manageable number for most to remember.

The entrepreneur will often have three to ten minutes to deliver the startup pitch. Three to ten minutes equates to eighteen to sixty seconds to speak to each slide. Even if the entrepreneur has more than five minutes, create the Investor Pitch Deck to use five minutes.

Why?

Because (sharing) less is (sharing) more. Attention spans are short. The entrepreneur wants the startup investor to have more time to ask questions. In order for the entrepreneur to get an investment on the first startup pitch to a startup investor in 100% unlikely. The goal is to

(1) pitch the startup Story to the startup investor, and (2) learn what is essential to the startup investor.

Let me reiterate this last point. You need to learn what is essential to the startup investor.

Every startup investor is different. Each startup investor has a distinct set of experiences, interests, and concerns. The entrepreneur must learn what these are to close the sale. A successful startup investor pitch is all about meeting the customer (investor) needs, NOT the sellers (entrepreneur) needs.

A startup investor pitch is Sales with a capital *S*. The sooner the entrepreneur learns this, the sooner you will do the job needed to close on the required fundraising.

Remember, the goal of this first meeting, what I refer to as the First-Date, is to get an invite to a Second-Date — NOT to get a check.

The entrepreneur wants the startup Story to carry the content value the startup investor needs to take the next step — an invitation for a Second-Date.

Best Practice #2: Assume the Investor sits 100' Away

I have seen so many Pitch Decks with text and numbers which are so small or of low contrast even when the startup investor sits five feet from the screen the slide is unreadable

What happens when a human sees the unreadable text? The visual cortex part of the brain goes into overdrive — and the hearing part of the brain all but shuts down.

We have all seen people attempt to read small text and numbers on a slide. The startup investor leans forward and starts squinting. As soon as the squinting begins, the listening all but stops. The startup investor focuses on an attempt to read the unreadable text.

The entrepreneur has lost the startup investor in under one second. Guess what? The entrepreneur may not regain the attention of the investor during the vital part of the Story on this slide.

Remember, the startup investor is meeting with the entrepreneur, NOT the Investor Pitch Deck. The Investor Pitch Deck slides are there to support the startup Story — NOT to tell the startup Story.

In some cases, if the entrepreneur is part of a startup accelerator or incubator, they will pitch to groups of startup investors in an auditorium setting. You MUST assume the startup investor sits up to 100 feet away.

Therefore, all text and numbers on a slide must be readable from 100 feet.

So how does the entrepreneur figure out the font size you should use on the slides? Well, there are some variables:

- The font you choose
- The font size you choose
- The contrast of the font color to the background

- The size of the presentation screen

- The darkness of the room

- The brightness of the display

- The average vision of the Investor

Formulas I found do not encompass all these variables. If the startup CEO presents on a 55-inch to a 100-inch diagonal screen, then the smallest text (a lower-case letter x) should be 4 to 8 inches tall at 100 feet. Text size of about 60 points with the regular Garamond font with black text on a white background will work well in a room with the lights at 50% full brightness level.

If you have a 55-inch TV at home, put the planned text on a PowerPoint slide and get as far away as possible. Text and numbers should be readable from 100-feet. If the text and figures are unreadable, use a larger font and increase the contrast or remove the text and numbers.

Best Practice #3: Use as Little Text as Possible

I will repeat this statement often. The startup investor meets with the entrepreneur to hear the startup Story, NOT to see the Investor Pitch Deck.

It is a documented fact — few humans can read and listen at the same time. Wait you say. I listen to music while I work all the time. Yes, you can hear music and other sounds while you work. However, your brain is unfocused on the music. Your mind focuses on reading the material in front of you.

If a stranger stopped a soundtrack of a new song with a lot of unique vocals while you were in a conversation, I would challenge you to recite to me the last five words you heard.

Why?

Because your brain focuses on the conversation, you were in with the live person. The background music vocals are little more than noise.

Any text put on a slide the startup investor will try to read. If the startup investor is reading, the startup investors are NOT LISTENING.

The entrepreneur wants the startup investor to be listening. Therefore, you want as little text as possible on each slide. In an ideal world, the slide title is the single piece of writing on the slide. Therefore, I teach the entrepreneur to use graphics to support the verbal startup Story.

If possible, any text on a slide should be single words. The goal is to have the startup investor examine the slide for no more than one-half to one second, then turn back to the entrepreneur to listen to the startup Story. Therefore, you want to pause the verbal part of the startup Story for up to one second when you transition to a new slide.

You can control the startup investor behavior through the practical use of the images and text on each slide.

For example, each slide should have the title of the slide, at the top left of the slide. For the Problem slide, you would transition from the

ANGEL INVESTORS TO VENTURE CAPITAL
10 SLIDES TO STARTUP FUNDING SUCCESS

Cover Slide to the Problem Slide, pause up to one second, then start the verbal part of the startup Story. The startup investors eyes focus on the title word PROBLEM at the top left of the slide due to it being the largest text on the slide and the word being at the top left of the slide. Then the investor examines the image on the slide and any other words and numbers. Dependent on the complexity and content of the Problem Slide image, this takes about one second. As the entrepreneur continues to speak, you will concisely, ideally in a single sentence, describe the problem. Next, with three to ten sentences, you will flush out the problem.

The image the entrepreneur uses on the slide should support the startup Story told WITHOUT the words present.

Few people, beyond the age of ten, desire to have anyone read aloud words on a slide — so please skip reading the slide text content aloud.

Other advantages exist for limited text on a slide:

- You can change the startup Story without modification of the slide

- If you share the slide deck with a startup investor, the startup investor will still have to get the entrepreneur on the phone, video conference, or back in front of the startup investor to have the entrepreneur tell the startup Story to other startup investor partners.

- If the slide deck were to fall into the hands of a competitor, there is limited value to the competitor.

I hope this has helped the entrepreneur understand the importance of limited text and numbers on the slides and reinforced the importance of the startup Story.

Best Practice #4: Never - Never Use Sentences!

Related to the earlier Best Practice of limiting the text and numbers on a slide, I need to ensure you understand this means there should NEVER, EVER BE SENTENCES on a slide.

The words you have should always be part of the slide title, a header, or a bullet point. NO SENTENCES — NO EXCEPTIONS!

Best Practice #5: Stick to High Contrast Colors

I know some of the entrepreneurs out there consider yourselves to be artists. You might have a hobby of painting, sketching, or drawing. However, when you create the Investor Pitch Deck, please leave most of these skills at home.

Remember, visual message support of the startup Story is the sole purpose of the Investor Pitch Deck. Earlier, I spoke to the importance of readability from 100 feet. High-contrast colors also aid in readability. Stay away from the pastel end of the color pallet. I recommend these colors.

- Black — #000000
- White - #FFFFFF

- Blue — #0000FF

- Green — #006400

- Red — #FF0000

Use a color checker for the background versus text and number color combination you choose to use to verify if the combination you have chosen will achieve a sharp contrast ratio. Below are a few sites you can do this on:

- <u>Colorable (Demo)</u> by Brent Jackson

- <u>Luminosity Color Contrast Ratio Analyzer</u> by Juicy Studio

- <u>Color Contrast Check</u> by Jonathan Snook

- <u>Color Contrast Checker</u> by WebAIM

- <u>Check My Colours</u> by Giovanni Scala

- <u>Color Safe</u> by Donielle Berg & Adrian Rapp

Limit the use of red colors. Human brains see the color read as ***Danger*** and ***Blood***. Skip this negative subconscious message by the minimal use of red in the Investor Pitch Deck.

Best Practice #6: Skip Busy Images

Quick. In the next image find the CD with the word *Encore.*

Figure 12- Cluttered Image

Miss it? Now in the following image find the CD with the word

Encore.

Figure 13- No Clutter Image

Hopefully, the reader realized they spent more time on the cluttered first image with many CDs than on the second image which had the single CD with the Encore name emblazoned on it.

The images you choose or create, need to be as focused as the words in the startup Story. Avoid the use of busy or too many images. Busy images cause the startup investor to stop listening to the entrepreneur and start staring at the cluttered image.

If the startup investor stares at the image, ***THE STARTUP INVESTOR IS NOT LISTENING TO YOU***.

You may be able to find the perfect image for each of the ten slides on the web. Remember, most of the images you see are the copyright works of the people who created these images.

The entrepreneur should avoid the use of images made by others without their written permission. One can get permission to use an image by the purchase of ***use-rights*** from the copyright holder via a website. Many websites sell use-rights for images. Some websites offer free-to-use for non-commercial uses and even free-to-use for any purpose. I chose not to share a list to image sites in this book as any list I share would be obsolete as soon as published.

The bottom line, please avoid the theft of an image from the web for use in the Investor Pitch Deck. Image theft is wrong, illegal and there is a good chance the startup investor has seen the image in another startup pitch deck. The use of a stolen image will reflect negatively on the entrepreneur.

For each of the ten slides in the Investor Pitch Deck, I recommend you find an image close to the message you want to convey. Mark up the image for the changes you want, then go to a website like www.fiverr.com and find a digital artist to create the ten images you will need for the ten slides. Several of my clients have followed this advice, and the custom images stand out when a startup investor views the Investor Pitch Deck. Original images place the presentation into a higher class versus the competition.

The other advantage to the construction of custom artwork is in the discovery of a digital artist who does excellent work at an affordable price. A digital artist can continue to work on future projects for the startup. The entrepreneur will need the skills of a digital artist for the construction of the Marketing, Sales, Customer Support, and future Investor Pitch Decks. The startup will need the digital artist skills for the website. Now is the correct time to put a name to the digital artist skill slot.

Best Practice #7: Use Pie Charts

Two slides in the Investor Pitch Deck exist in which the entrepreneur should consider the use of a Pie Chart.

- Monetization (Slide #7)
- Ask (Slide #10)

Most entrepreneurs will use tables full of numbers to share the content of these two slides with the startup investor. Tables full of numbers are a bad idea for the same reason lots of words are a bad idea.

If the startup investor is reading the slide, the startup investor is NOT LISTENING TO YOU!

I will get into the content of each of the slides in later chapters. For now, remember when you get to these slides in the Investor Pitch Deck, think pie chart!

Best Practice #8: Use a Side-by-Side Bar Chart

One slide in the Investor Pitch Deck exists in which the entrepreneur will want to use a Side-by-Side Bar Chart.

1. Financials (Slide #8)

Every Financial Slide I see in a first attempt Investor Pitch Deck is a giant table of numbers:

Revenue	FY 13/14	FY 14/15	FY 15/16	FY 16/17	FY 17/18 Budget
Annual Financial Commitment	$866,269	$898,000	$1,030,866	$1,048,102	$1,119,830
Religious School Fees & Adult Ed (a)	$202,307	$180,000	$154,282	$146,620	$121,500
General Contributions (b)	$186,356	$365,000	$366,297	$274,615	$401,380
Grants	$119,448	$67,500	$78,750	$78,950	$107,500
Other (c)	$25,849	$23,800	$31,964	$51,510	$24,080
Total Revenue	$1,400,229	$1,534,300	$1,662,159	$1,599,797	$1,774,290
Expenses					
Rabbinic Services, Support	$470,467	$486,171	$485,174	$438,284	$455,100
Religious Events	$85,679	$85,460	$89,769	$76,763	$79,200
Education	$244,491	$254,747	$226,643	$285,291	$301,804
Administration	$381,844	$368,096	$391,829	$417,061	$490,025
Facility	$231,055	$209,780	$233,079	$260,588	$252,192
URJ Membership Dues	$57,508	$86,300	$62,736	$62,209	$62,208
Tikkun Olam	$32,080	$41,800	$45,122	$54,472	$50,500
Total Expenses	$1,503,124	$1,532,354	$1,534,352	$1,594,668	$1,691,029
Revenue(Expenses) in Excess of Expenses(Revenue)	-$102,895	$1,946	$127,807	$5,129	$83,261

Figure 14 - Bad Way to Show Financials

Display the Financials Slide in this unwise format and the entrepreneur has lost the startup investor. The startup investor is reading the table, which means the startup investor is NOT LISTENING TO YOU. Each startup investor is busy in their search for their favorite number in this massive table of numbers.

Now instead, imagine the entrepreneur took the crucial parts of the same information and displayed it in a Side-by-Side Bar Chart:

Figure 15 - Good Way to Show Financials

The essential financials points are all here. The startup investor will see numbers in the millions of dollars. The slide will have a red arrow which points to the date of the break-even financial point. The slide will show the critical metrics of Revenue, Expenses and Customer Traffic growth. These are the crucial points to which the entrepreneur will speak. There should be no unnecessary words or numbers to clutter up the startup Story.

Which design do you think will help the entrepreneur keep the startup investor focused? Which slide will answer critical startup investor questions?

Best Practice #9: Use a Table

One slide in the Investor Pitch Deck exists in which the entrepreneur will want to use a Table.

- Competition (Slide #6)

Many Investor Pitch Decks skip the mention of competition. Not speaking to the startup competition is a big mistake.

When the entrepreneur creates the Competition Slide, often only lists two to three competitors. A list of two or three competitors is not the way to correctly build a Competition Slide.

The Competition Slide is the one slide where the use of a Table is a MUST. Here is an example:

COMPETITION	YOUR COMPANY	Caresync	McKesson	Oculus Health	Thorough care	Chronic Care Mngm LLC	Avicenna Medical
ALERTS	✓	✓	⊘	⊘	⊘	⊘	⊘
TELENURSING	✓	✓	✓	✓	⊘	✓	⊘
DEVICES (Wearable and in-home)	✓	✓	✓	⊘	⊘	⊘	⊘
DASHBOARD	✓	⊘	⊘	⊘	✓	⊘	⊘
Sharing/Communication	✓	✓	⊘	⊘	⊘	⊘	⊘
Care Plan Management	✓	⊘	✓	⊘	⊘	✓	✓
Medication Management	✓	✓	⊘	⊘	⊘	⊘	⊘
Chronic Care Management	✓	✓	✓	✓	✓	✓	✓
EHR	✓	✓	✓	✓	✓	✓	✓

Figure 16 - Table for Competition Slide

I will go into more detail when I cover the Competition Slide in a later chapter. However, remember the Table format allows the entrepreneur to focus on the crucial message points without the inclusion of unneeded information.

Best Practice #10: Include URL to All 3rd Party Data

The Market Slide always has specific data about the Total Available Market (TAM) and Serviceable Addressable Market (SAM). Most startup investors will examine these number with a jaded eye. Where did the entrepreneur get these numbers? Did the entrepreneur invent the numbers or get the numbers from a respected source?

There is a sure-fire way to turn off the startup investors bulls**t reaction to the Market numbers the entrepreneur presents.

Include a URL link to the one or more third-party reports from which the entrepreneur extracted the market data.

Make oral reference to the fact you have the URL at the bottom of the Market Slide should the startup investor desire to later review the source data. If the entrepreneur uses well known, reputable sources, the startup investors bulls**t meter should fall to zero.

Best Practice #11: Never Use Animated Slides

I know some entrepreneurs who are PowerPoint power users and have learned all the ins-and-outs of the construction of animated slides. What is an animated slide? On animated slides, words and objects appear and disappear on the base slide either automatically or each time the entrepreneur taps on the arrow key or touchpad.

While animated slides may be pretty to some people, animated slides are a distraction to most startup investors. Guess why? The startup investor watches all the fancy animation. Guess what this means?

While the startup investor watches the fancy slideshow, the startup investor is NOT LISTENING TO YOU!

Unless the entrepreneur wants a PowerPoint Slide Deck construction job in a big startup, remove all animations!

Besides the animation distraction, guess what else happens? Animated slides sometimes break. I have seen animated slides break more times than I can remember.

Sometimes the entrepreneur hits the clicker too soon to fire off an animated slide. Then you must stop the oral presentation while you rewind to the earlier slide. You have lost the startup investor, and you look bad. Was the animated slide worth it even if the animation launched too early?

Sometimes, when you convert the Investor Pitch Deck to a PDF, all sorts of weird results can happen.

Usually, the entrepreneur prints the pre-animation version of the Investor Pitch Deck. If just the pre-animation slide is in the PDF, then critical information is not in the PDF. One does not want to share an incomplete Investor Pitch Deck with startup investors.

Other times a multi-slide animation blows up the PDF conversion process, and no PDF file is output. One solution is to create a copy of the PowerPoint Investor Pitch Deck and remove all the animation. Now you must support two Investor Pitch Decks.

The best solution is to skip animations in the Investor Pitch Deck. Easy solution and less work. No animations in the Investor Pitch Deck equals a Win-Win.

Best Practice #12: Never Show a Live Website or App

You have this cool SaaS (Software-as-a-Service) business, and you are proud of the website or app. You are about to pitch to a startup investor, or a room full of startup investors, and you feel if you show how cool the website or app is, this will help get an investment.

You are wrong if this is what you think. The entrepreneur's desire to showcase the website or app is an unwise First-Date activity.

Remember, the entrepreneur has three to ten minutes to pitch. The demo of a website, no matter how simple or abbreviated, will often cause the startup investor pitch to run more than the allotted time.

Web connections often break or are slow. As soon as you click a button to show a website or app, you have lost the startup investor. Mobile phones come out of the pockets of startup investors while the site or app begins to spin up.

Nobody cares about a demo at the First-Date stage. Demos are for a Second-Date or later meeting. When the startup investor is ready to see the work product, they will ask for a product demo.

Bottom line: Say NO to a demo the website or app while at the First-Date startup pitch event.

Best Practice #13: Never Show a Video

A few entrepreneurs will think a video is a neat way to display a product or service. A neat video may be a great technique to help sell to a customer. However, avoid videos at a First-Date or even a Second-Date startup investor meeting.

When the entrepreneur shows a video that most startup investors are uninterested in at this point in the engagement, the entrepreneur will lose the startup investor attention. Investors have the same reaction to a video on a First-Date that most people do to an auto-play video ad on a website URL one visits. Annoying!

Just like with animated slides or a URL to a website or app, videos are at best problematic. Videos are expensive in money and time perspective to construct — like a movie at the theater. Lots of planning, staging, editing, re-editing and more go into the construction of a 15-60-second product video.

Again, the startup investor is uninterested in how slick a video the entrepreneur can produce. The startup investor is more interested in the startup Story the entrepreneur tells about the startup.

Keep the Investor Pitch Deck simple. Just say NO to videos in the Investor Pitch Deck.

Best Practice #14: Use a Master Slide

I saved this Best Practice for near the end. The best way to achieve consistency in the construction in the Investor Pitch Deck is to use a

Master Slide. Whether you use Microsoft PowerPoint, Apples Keynote, or Google Slides, each has Master Slide capabilities.

You can set the default font sizes, colors, background colors, headers, footers in a Master Slide. Use of a Master Slide also allows the startup to brand the startup name and logo onto each page for a consistent look.

Each of these tools also allows one to export a PDF version of the Investor Pitch Deck to share and for review purposes.

Since you have bought my book, I have a reward for you. Go to the last section of this book which is titled Resources. Here you will find a link which will get you a deep discount on a set of Investor Pitch Deck Master Slide templates I sell as part of a bigger package.

Since you have already bought my book, I want to help you take the next step in the implementation of these Best Practices in the fastest and easiest way possible!

In summary, please use a Master Slide method to create the Investor Pitch Deck. I promise you will save lots of time, have a consistent look and feel and be happy you did.

Best Practice #15: Practice - Practice - Practice

The final Best Practices lesson is - Practice.

Practice is crucial to a successful Investor Pitch Deck presentation. It is better to practice more than you think you should than to practice insufficiently. Most entrepreneurs practice:

- Too little practice

- Do not practice aloud

- Do not practice in front of a live Investor

- Practice only in front of Friends, Family, and other team members

Most entrepreneurs have limited to no experience at public speaking or startup investor presentations. The entrepreneur may be able to create an earth-shattering Investor Pitch Deck. However, if the entrepreneur is unable to deliver the oral startup Story, there is no winning startup investor pitch.

How does the entrepreneur learn how to master the oral delivery of the startup investor pitch?

Practice - Practice - Practice. No other action replaces tons of practice. To practice your startup pitch in your head is an unwise practice technique. The entrepreneur must practice as if they were to present to a room full of startup investors. To practice in front of one to two people and then to a crowd is a requirement to be prepared to pitch to a startup investor.

The entrepreneur must also dress for the practice sessions. Never practice in your underwear or sweats. The minimum requirement is to practice dressed in business casual attire. One should also practice in formal business attire.

Buy a tripod you can mount a mobile phone on and record every practice. Here is one on Amazon which works well, is portable and works with most any phone:

https://www.amazon.com/DIGIANT-Aluminum-Universal-Smartphone-Smartphones/dp/B018ICYNKY/

Make a Pitch Deck Verbal Practice Checklist:

- How many Ah, Oh, Like, Um did you use. Count each and write the number on the checklist.

- Did you freeze and forget the startup Story on any slide?

- Did your eyes focus on the startup investors or did you stare at the slides?

- Did you stand up straight or slouch?

- Did you stand in one spot or move around?

- Did you use your hands when speaking or hold your hands at your side or put your hands in your pants pockets?

- Was your tone of voice monotonic or animated?

- Did you speak slow or quick?

- How much time did you spend on each slide?
  - Slide 1: xx seconds
  - Slide 2: xx seconds
  - Slide N: xx seconds

- Was the time spent on each slide uniform?

- Did you enunciate each word in a clear fashion with an audible gap between each word?

- Did you use **pregnant pauses** to emphasize critical points?
- Did you smile?

Many more items exist on the checklist. Since you have bought my book, I have a reward for you. Go to the last section of this book titled RESOURCES. Here is a link to a FREE copy of my **Investor Pitch Deck Verbal Practice Checklist**.

https://ideatogrowth.com/contact-free-download-investor-pitch-deck-verbal-practice-checklist/

You need to practice in front of ten plus people also. For the presentation practices you want random startup investor feedback on, you can search for a local meetup called 1-Million Cups. 1-Million Cups is a USA organization targeted to help local startup entrepreneurs. Click the below link to find out more.

https://www.1millioncups.com/

Another great organization where you want honest feedback on your speaking skills, more than the startup pitch content, I recommend you join Toast Masters (https://www.toastmasters.org). Toast Masters is an organization whose purpose in life is to help you become a better speaker — and the attendees will help you become a better speaker. At each session, you speak, members provide honest feedback and tips for improvement. Toast Masters is a great organization to join.

I now conclude my Best Practices for Investor Pitch Deck Construction. This section of the book is the one I will update on a regular basis with more Best Practices and tips, so if you have bought the Kindle version, be sure you check here for updates to the book on a regular basis.

Please take a moment and click on this next link to share your preferred email address. I will email you when I update the book.

Yes, please email me when you update the book. Here is my preferred Email address:

https://www.ideatogrowth.com/contact-book-owner-10-slides-to-startup-funding-success/

Also, be sure to check out the Resources page for helpful downloads! There is also a link to save you dozens of hours building your own Investor Pitch Deck Slide template. For book buyers I include a discount code that will save you $$$.

Click RESOURCES to jump to the download page now.

ANGEL INVESTORS TO VENTURE CAPITAL
10 SLIDES TO STARTUP FUNDING SUCCESS

In the next chapter, I will speak about the first slide of our Investor Pitch Deck - The Cover Slide.

Chapter Quiz

Q1: How many slides should a great investor presentation have?
[ ] 5 [ ] 10 [ ] 20 [ ]25 [ ] 30 [ ] As many as you want

Q2: Name the titles for each slide of the main pitch deck.

Q3: Describe the "Rule of 3" and how it relates to pitching.

Q4: Each slide should have lots of text in full sentence format.
[ ] True [ ] False

Q5: From what distance should the audience be able to easily read all
text and numbers on each slide? [ ] 10' [ ] 25' [ ] 50' [ ] 100'

Q6: Colorful pastels are the best color choice for fonts. [ ] Yes [ ] No

Q7: Always show a detailed table of financials. [ ] Yes [ ] No

Q8: Always include a video to spiff up your pitch. [ ] Yes [ ] No

Q9: Using images you download from Google is OK. [ ] Yes [ ] No

Q10: You should make each slide 100% custom. [ ] Yes [ ] No

Q11: Practice your verbal pitch in your head for 10 hours to get ready.
[ ] Yes [ ] No

Q12: When delivering your pitch, sit or stand straight and hold your
hands and arms at your side is the best method. [ ] Yes [ ] No

Q13: Demo of your product as part of your pitch. [ ] Yes [ ] No

Answers:

https://www.ideatogrowth.com/Answers-10-Slides-to-Startup-Funding-Success/#best-practices

Chapter Notes

The Most Overlooked Slide

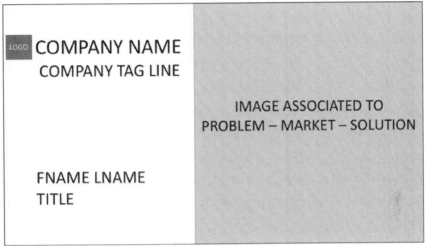

Figure 17 - Cover Slide, The Most Overlook Slide

The Cover Slide — Why Is It Important?

The Cover Slide, the first slide of the Investor Pitch Deck, is the slide I refer to as the Most Overlooked Slide in the Investor Pitch Deck.

Why do I say this?

I have lots of experience reviewing Investor Pitch Decks.

With the Cover Slide, the entrepreneur will introduce the startup, themselves and answer to the first unspoken startup investor question *Who are you and why am I spending time with you?* (Slide 1).

The Cover Slide sets the Investor's first impression of the entrepreneur and the Story they are about to hear.

Next, the Cover Slide, combined with your attire, stride, and smile create the all-important first impression.

Lastly, the Cover Slide is of the same import as the cover and title of any book you might examine to buy. The image(s), the word(s), the color(s), the font(s), and layout all set the expectation of what a startup investor will find inside. If the author of the book has made unwise choices in the design of the cover of the book, will you buy the book?

Think of the Cover Slide in the same way as you would if you were about to decide what to wear on a First-Date. When on a date, one wants to create a great first impression, right? Do you put on some dirty clothes you picked up off the floor or put on clean clothes? Coordination of your attire is what one does, right?

Just like a First-Date, the Cover Slide can make-or-break how the next nine slides connect with startup investors.

In many cases, the Cover Slide will be visible for the most extended period of the presentation. If the startup CEO presents to a group of startup investors, the Cover Slide will often be visible before you step onto the stage.

The Cover Slide should get the startup investor interested in the startup Story you are about to share. If you have an inadequate Cover Slide, the startup investor could reach for a mobile phone to entertain themselves. Best case, an inadequately designed Cover Slide will have the startup investor think *OMG - How are you about to bore to me?*

Time to learn about the Cover startup Story content.

The Cover Slide - The Startup Story Content

First, write down the critical oral points the startup investor should want to hear when the entrepreneur begins the Investor Pitch Deck presentation.

Just like on a First-Date, these first words will often set the tone for the rest of the engagement. Keep your opening statement simple.

What investor questions should the verbal Story answer?

- State your full name
- State your position (title) in the startup
- State your startup name
- State why you are here to present to the Investor
- Thank the startup investor for their attendance

However, before the entrepreneur begins the startup pitch, you must get the attention of the audience. What should be the first words out of your mouth?

At a group startup pitch event, there is an excellent technique to shut down conversations in the crowd. Start by speaking:

Good Day. Is everyone ready to get started?

Wait for everyone to look away from computers, phones, and documents. Wait for every person present to focus on the entrepreneur will face. It may take several seconds for the entrepreneur to get the attention of everyone in the audience. It is essential for the entrepreneur to hold their breath and wait.

Most people hate silence. When there is no noise or other sounds, even the most distracted person will look up to see what is up.

If necessary, repeat the phrase:

Good Day. Is everyone ready to get started?

When the last person stares at the entrepreneur, this is when the entrepreneur starts the presentation.

Now let us discuss how to Craft and Deliver the Cover startup Story.

The Cover Slide — Craft the Startup Story

Allow me to provide one example of the Cover Slide oral startup pitch which would work well.

Good Day. Is everyone ready to get started?

Good (morning, afternoon, evening). Thank you for sharing your valuable time with me today. My name is (Your Full Name). I am the founder and CEO of (company). Next to me is my co-founder (Full Name) the CTO. Today, I (we) will share the startup Story behind (company) and the plan to bring an incredible solution to solve the market problem.

Wow. The entrepreneur has the startup investor focused on them, and the startup Story told has answered the startup investors first unspoken startup investor question. The startup investor waits in eager anticipation of the next words to come out of the entrepreneur's mouth.

SLIDE 1 — THE COVER SLIDE

The first words out of your mouth, and the delivery and energy level, will set the tone for the presentation. Follow these rules for a successful performance.

- You MUST smile.
- You should animate your body and hands.
- Your vocal sound should be audible to the people furthest from you.
- Your voice should reek of high energy, a healthy level of excitement and confidence.
- You should take 18-30 seconds for the oral delivery

Another plus of the Cover Slide oral presentation is the presentation of this slide allows you to calm any jitters and get you in the zone for a flawless performance. Even those who have given talks hundreds or even thousands of times in front of startup investors like to have a starter ramp to get into the groove at the start of a presentation. The Cover Slide is the starter ramp helps the entrepreneur get into the groove.

Now it is time to discuss how to create the Cover Slide.

The Cover Slide - Create the Slide

Most Cover Slides I see from entrepreneurs are bland. Usually, text on a solid background. Excuse me; I fell asleep from the dull Cover Slide!

ANGEL INVESTORS TO VENTURE CAPITAL
10 SLIDES TO STARTUP FUNDING SUCCESS

Other Cover Slides I have seen include a busy image or too much text. Neither of these examples delivers the positive first impression the entrepreneur wants to give to any startup investor.

The Cover Slide should convey to the startup investor a solid idea of the product or service of the startup.

For example, say the product is a mobile-focused advertising service. The entrepreneur might convey the service with an image which includes some happy millennials with smiles who gaze at their cell phones. With no text at all, you have provided the startup investor has a strong clue to the startup product or service. The product or service has to do with interaction among young people their cell phones.

In the Best Practices section, I wrote about the importance of text minimization. A limited quantity of text should exist on the Cover Slide.

What investor questions should the slide answer?

- Company Name
- Company Tagline
- Company Logo
- Presenters Full Name
- Presenters Position (Title)
- Image(s) which conveys the startup purpose and ties to the startup Story

SLIDE 1 — THE COVER SLIDE

The reader might think it would be obvious the startup name must be on the Cover Slide. However, in many presentations I have witnessed, the Cover Slide lacked the startup name!

Remember, like all text, the startup name should be readable from 100 feet away.

Why?

The startup CEO will sometimes present in an auditorium where startup investors sit 100 feet away. If much of the text is unreadable, the startup investor will lose interest in the startup pitch. The entrepreneur has lost startup investors.

All text on any slide should be in sharp contrast when laid on top of any image or color. Again, the focus is to ensure all text is readable.

If a co-founder presents with you, include the co-founder's full name and title. If the startup is technical, and the CEO is not the non-technical co-founder, I urge both the startup CEO and the CTO be present at all startup investor presentations.

If the startup success is rooted in technology, most startup investors will have immediate questions about the technology. The strength of the technical co-founder will go a long way in the determination of if the startup can navigate the First-Date and get an invite for a Second-Date.

Several items I recommend not be present on the Cover Slide.

- The Date
- The title *Investor Presentation*

- Phone Numbers

- LinkedIn Profiles

- Company Website

Leave the date of the presentation off the Cover Slide. It is too easy to forget to update the Cover Slide date when a sudden opportunity to present to a new startup investor occurs. Incorrect date on the slide appears unprofessional.

The title Investor Presentation is unneeded information.

The entrepreneur's phone number is unneeded information. When you do the post-presentation follow-up email, you can share your cell phone number.

The same is true of the entrepreneurs LinkedIn URL.

Never put the startup URL on the Cover Slide. I have seen startup investors open a laptop or pull out a cell phone and visit the startup website as the entrepreneur starts the startup investor pitch. The entrepreneur wants all startup investors to listen to the startup pitch. The startup investor should be 100% focused on the entrepreneur as they share the startup Story.

Now, examine both a good and a poor example of how to create a Cover Slide.

Figure 18 - Cover Slide - Bad Example

Can you list the recommended content this creator included?

- An image tries to create the reference to the startup Story

- The startup name, tagline, and logo

- The entrepreneur's name and title

What did the creator of this Cover Slide get wrong?

- They added text Investor Presentation

- They added a phone number

- They added an email

- They added a LinkedIn URL

- They added the website URL

- They added a date

- The image appears unrelated to the service described by the startup name or tagline.

Bottom line, this example of an inadequate Cover Slide includes several items unuseful to the startup investor at this engagement stage.

Some of the font sizes look too small to pass the 100-foot readability test.

What would be my recommended changes?

Figure 19 - Cover Slide - Good Example

- Remove the phone number
- Remove the email
- Remove the LinkedIn URL
- Remove the website URL
- Remove the text startup investor Presentation
- Remove the date
- Make the startup name a bigger font for 100 feet readability
- Make the entrepreneur's name and title readable from 100 feet

- Change the image to show two seniors, one male, one female, to reflect the startup focus better

Now the startup investor will glance at the slide for one second, get the critical information for a good first guess as to what the startup is about, and then gaze back onto the entrepreneurs face. This action by the startup investor shows the entrepreneur has created an excellent Cover Slide.

Now it is time to discuss the Cover Backup Slides.

The Cover Slide - Backup Slides

For the first time, I will dive into the subject of backup slides. However, each of the 10-Slide Investor Pitch Deck should have related backup content. In each slides chapter, I will have a subchapter which details some of the back-ups slides one might want to create and include in the backup slide section.

The backup slide section begins with a Table of Contents, which is the eleventh slide. List the title of each backup slide underneath the first title of each of the ten Investor Pitch Deck slides.

The Cover Slide backup slides should include:

- Startup website URL
- Startup physical address
- Startup mail address
- Startup phone number
- Contact details on the speaker(s)

- Email

- Cell Phone

- LinkedIn URL

Remember, the goal of the Cover slide is to introduce the startup and the entrepreneur.

Time to look at a short Cover Slide checklist.

The Cover Slide - Construction Checklist

Remember these crucial points about the Cover Slide startup Story.

- ☐ Use a Master Template
- ☐ Startup Name
- ☐ Startup Tagline
- ☐ Startup Logo
- ☐ Presenter Full Name
- ☐ Presenter Position (Title)
- ☐ All text is Legible from 100 Feet (33 Meters)
- ☐ Bold Colors (no pastels or light colors)
- ☐ Images related to the startup Mission or Product
- ☐ Leave off the slide: Email Address
- ☐ Leave off the slide: LinkedIn URL
- ☐ Leave off the slide: startup Website URL
- ☐ Leave off the slide: All Phone Numbers
- ☐ Leave off the slide: Twitter Address
- ☐ Leave off the slide: Facebook URL
- ☐ Leave off the slide: All Dates
- ☐ Leave off the slide: Presenters Face Image

You can download the Complete Investor Pitch Deck Checklist - **100% FREE** - Click the link below while connected to WiFi.

https://www.ideatogrowth.com/contact-free-download-investor-pitch-deck-checklist

ANGEL INVESTORS TO VENTURE CAPITAL
10 SLIDES TO STARTUP FUNDING SUCCESS

The Cover Slide - Executive Summary

The Cover Slide Story and Slide include the below info.

- Use of a Master template (Slide)

- Startup Name (Slide & Story)

- Startup Tagline (Slide & Story)

- Startup Logo (Slide)

- Presenters Full Name (Slide & Story)

- Presenters Title (Slide & Story)

- An image suggesting the content of the Story to come (Slide)

- Deliver the Cover Story in 18-30 seconds (Story)

- Minimize Text - Use Images to Tell the startup Story (Slide)

- The text is Legible from 100 Feet (33 Meters) (Slide)

- Bold Colors (no pastels or light colors) (Slide)

In the next chapter, I will speak about the second part of the startup Story — The Problem Slide.

Also, be sure to check out the Resources page for helpful downloads! There is also a link to save you dozens of hours building your own Investor Pitch Deck Slide template. For book buyers I include a discount code that will save you $$$.

Click RESOURCES to jump to the download page now.

SLIDE 1 — THE COVER SLIDE

Chapter Quiz

Q1: Cover slide has the speakers phone number and [ ] Yes [ ] No

Q2: The Cover slide should have a picture that brings the Problem, and the Solution to the audience's mind. [ ] Yes [ ] No

Q3: Always put all the presenter's social media URL's on the Cover slide so the investors know how to reach out. [ ] Yes [ ] No

Q4: Cover slide title "Investor Presentation". [ ] Yes [ ] No

Q5: Name 8 things that should be on the "backup" slide to the Cover slide.

Q6: From what distance should the audience be able to easily read any text or numbers on the Cover slide? [ ] 10' [ ] 25' [ ] 50' [ ] 100'

Q7: How many seconds do you have for the verbal story related to the Cover slide in a 6-minute total verbal pitch time?

Q8: Always deliver the pitch in a soft voice so the audience must lean in and listen closely to hear you. [ ] Yes [ ] No

Q9: Never use black text on a white background. [ ] Yes [ ] No

Q10: You should never smile when pitching. [ ] Yes [ ] No

Q11: The Cover Page should only have your company name, logo, tagline, presenters name & title and a related image(s). [ ] Yes [ ] No

Answers:

https://www.ideatogrowth.com/answers-10-slides-to-startup-funding-success/#slide-1-the-cover-slide

Chapter Notes

The Big, Hairy Problem

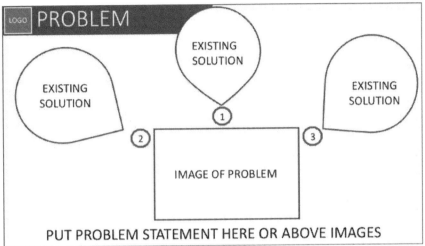

Figure 20 - The Problem Slide

The Problem Slide — Why Is It Important?

Why do startup investors want to hear about the Problem now?

With the Cover Slide, the entrepreneur introduced the startup, themselves and answered the first unspoken startup investor question:

Who are you and why am I spending time with you? (Slide 1).

Now the mind of the startup investor asks:

What is the Big, Hairy Problem This Startup has Targeted? (Slide 2)

Noticed I said ***Big, Hairy Problem***. Why did I choose these words? No startup investor wants to hear about solutions to minor problems.

ANGEL INVESTORS TO VENTURE CAPITAL
10 SLIDES TO STARTUP FUNDING SUCCESS

Small Problems equals few customers and low revenues. Small problems mean startup investors will not have big paydays. If a startup investor sees no future big payday, the startup investor does not desire to spend time with the entrepreneur.

Every startup investor wants to invest in companies with market target sizes of USD 1B+. Startup investors big paydays happen when the startup can find a buyer to pay ten times or more than the startup investor paid for the startup stock. Small market products and services often have too small of a return for most startup investors. If the market size for the startup the entrepreneur starts is less than USD 1B, the entrepreneur will face considerable investment difficulty.

How does the entrepreneur know if they have found a Big, Hairy, Problem Market?

Two words. Market Research.

Later in Slide 3, I discuss Market Research and its associated Market Slide — The Market Slide.

However, if I may, I have a few words of wisdom and guidance.

Please do not waste a startup investors time with an Investor Pitch Deck presentation unless the Market for the Problem is north of USD 1B. If the entrepreneur wastes the time of a startup investor with a startup pitch to fundraise for a small market opportunity, the entrepreneur will not get an audience with the startup investor a second time — a time when the entrepreneur might have a big Market Product Solution for a Big, Hairy Problem.

Kenneth Ervin Young   80   Idea To Growth LLC

Time to learn about the Problem startup Story content.

The Problem Slide - The Startup Story Content

First, write down the critical oral points the startup investor should want to hear when the entrepreneur describes the Problem the startup will solve.

What investor questions should the verbal Story answer?

- Describe the Problem by use of a relatable example

- Describe the Problem by use of a question

- Answer the question which describes the Problem

I recommend an excellent presentation technique for the Problem Slide and to get startup investor engagement.

Start the Problem Slide presentation with a question.

Start with a Question

The startup investor may have a riveted gaze in the direction of the entrepreneur, but is the startup investors mind focused elsewhere? Studies have shown when someone asks a question, the part of the brain responsible for an answer becomes more active. A question from the entrepreneur will push away most other thoughts in the startup investors mind.

A well-chosen oral question or two when you continue the startup pitch with the Problem Slide will focus the startup investor on the startup Story.

The question(s) and oral delivery are critical. Ideally, the Problem is one in which the startup investor can relate to personal experience.

Another engagement technique is to get the physical engagement by the startup investor when the entrepreneur asks the question. How does a question asked by the entrepreneur get physical startup investor engagement?

Simple. Include the oral precursor **By a Show of Hands** in front of the question.

Any other mental distractions in a startup investors head will disappear when a startup investor must choose whether to lift a hand.

After the question, the entrepreneur will answer the question. The question and its answer should relate to the **Big, Hairy Problem**.

Allow me to provide an example from one of the Startup Accelerator companies I have coached. The name of the startup is Trucks-on-Demand (TOD).

The Problem TOD solves how to help the consumer get an oversized purchase home right away — not days or weeks after purchase when the store can fit a delivery into the schedule.

TOD is a SaaS startup. Open the TOD phone app. The app works like the Uber and Lyft apps. Users can see TOD drivers who own trucks or vans near the store where a consumer purchases an oversized item. The consumer answers a few simple questions and, in a few minutes a TOD driver shows up, puts the oversized item into the truck, follows the buyer home, and unloads the oversized piece into its final spot in the buyer's home. The TOD app user gets real-time delivery service for USD 20, plus USD 1 per mile. Pretty slick, right?

Now let us discuss how to Craft and Deliver the Problem startup Story.

The Problem Slide — Craft the Startup Story

Allow me to provide one example of the Problem Slide oral startup pitch which would work well.

Good Day. I have a question for you. By a quick show of hands, how many of you have gone to a store and bought an oversized item — a TV, Couch, Bed or Lawn Mower — and the store schedules the home delivery to occur about six weeks? (Hands go up). Every one of us, right? Most of us would prefer the purchase to follow us home, right? (Most people nod in the affirmative or verbalize Yes). The desire to get those oversized items back home immediately is why we started Trucks on Demand.

This Problem startup Story got my attention. Did this Problem startup Story get your attention?

I hope this illustrates how the vocalization of the Problem with a great question the startup investor can relate to is crucial. Most startup investors can remember a personal experience where a service like TOD would have made life better.

As the entrepreneur, your challenge is to create a similar Problem startup Story and Problem Slide the startup investor can relate to for your startup.

Remember, the entrepreneur wants to create the Problem startup Story for the benefit of the startup investor. Done correctly, the Problem Slide can also be a crucial slide in the Customer Sales Pitch.

Now it is time to discuss how to create the Problem Slide.

The Problem Slide - Create the Slide

Most Problem Slides I see from entrepreneurs are in a state of disorder about content and format. In some cases, the Problem slide does not describe the Problem with clarity. I have sat in many startup investor pitches in which the startup CEO presented 10+ slides, and I still had no idea of the problem the startup addresses. Please avoid this scenario!

The Problem Slide should convey to the startup investor a clear image of the *Big, Hairy Problem*.

What investor questions should the slide answer?

- Include the slide title: PROBLEM
- Image(s) describe the Problem and tie to the startup Story

Let us start with how not to build a Problem Slide.

In the next slide example, I show what I see on most Problem Slides from startup teams — a bunch of words. This example does a good job of describing the problem that the company is tackling.

However, the startup CEO is likely going to verbalize the same words to the startup investors. The startup CEO is violating my best practice of not making slides that they read to the audience.

HOW DO I GET MY NEW COUCH HOME?

1. WAIT 8+ WEEKS FOR THE STORE TO DELIVER?
2. TIE THE TV ON TOP OF MY VW BUG?
3. CALL A NEIGHBOR WITH A TRUCK?

Figure 21 - Problem Slide - Bad Example

For an excellent slide example, let us refer to the startup TOD.

For TOD, one might create a Problem Slide with a background image of an unhappy consumer with a question on their face look. The buyer would gaze at the oversized purchase. The buyer's facial expression would say ***How the heck do I get this giant box home?***

Three clouds represent ***thoughts*** above the consumers head.

The first thought cloud has an image of a grizzled delivery driver who drives a beat-up, old pickup truck.

The second thought cloud has an image of the consumers small vehicle with the big box strapped onto the roof with a rope.

The third thought cloud has the image of a calendar which shows a six-week delivery marked with a big red circle around the distant date.

The Problem Slide might look like the slide shown next.

Figure 22 - Problem Slide - Good Example

With limited text, the startup investor has a clear mental image as to the ***Big Hairy, Problem*** the startup is there to solve.

Do not give in to the temptation to provide a tease the Solution as part of the Problem Slide. The entrepreneur should build anticipation for the Solution Slide.

Now it is time to discuss the Problem Backup Slides.

The Problem Slide - Backup Slides

The Problem Slide backup slides should include:

- A separate slide with images for each listed part of the problem and a different slide for each essential unlisted problem

Remember, the goal of the Problem slide is to keep the declaration of the problem as simple as possible.

The Problem Slide - Construction Checklist

Remember these crucial points about the Problem Slide startup Story.

- ☐ Use a Master Template
- ☐ Title: PROBLEM
- ☐ Start the Problem Slide startup Story with a Question
- ☐ Make the Question relatable to the Audience
- ☐ Get physical audience engagement: ***By a show of Hands***
- ☐ Custom Images are a Good Choice
- ☐ Match Images to the startup Story
- ☐ All text is LEGIBLE from 100 Feet (33 Meters)
- ☐ Bold Colors (no pastels or light colors)
- ☐ Have backup slides with more Problem details

You can download the Complete Investor Pitch Deck Checklist - ***100% FREE*** - Click the link below while connected to WiFi.

https://www.ideatogrowth.com/contact-free-download-investor-pitch-deck-checklist

The Problem Slide - Executive Summary

The Problem Slide Story and Slide include the below info.

- Use of a Master template (Slide)

- PROBLEM for the slide title (Slide)

- Image(s) which support the Problem Story (Slide)

- The verbal Problem Story starts with a question to which the audience (Investor) can relate (Story)

- The startup CEO gets the audience (Investor) to have physical engagement by the words *By a Show of Hands* (Story)

- The startup CEO answers the question the entrepreneur asked related to the problem

- The Problem Slide image(s) help describe the Problem (Slide)

- Deliver the Problem Story in 18-30 seconds (Story)

- Minimize Text - Use Images to Tell the startup Story (Slide)

- The text is Legible from 100 Feet (33 Meters) (Slide)

- Bold Colors (no pastels or light colors) (Slide)

In the next chapter, I will speak about the third part of the startup Story — The Market Slide.

Chapter Quiz

Q1: You should always start the Problem slide with a verbal question?
[ ] Yes [ ] No

Q2: The title of the Problem slide should be "Challenge".
[ ] Yes [ ] No

Q3: The Problem slide must have a lengthy list of problems your Solution is solving. [ ] Yes [ ] No

Q4: The Problem slide should include an image(s) clearly indicative of the problem, a short single line statement of the problem and no other words. [ ] Yes [ ] No

Q5: Use a google search to find your best image. [ ] Yes [ ] No

Q6: What should the Problem backup slide include?

Q7: Use pastel and low contrast colors for impact. [ ] Yes [ ] No

Q8: It's best practice to have multiple Problem slides to accurately depict the problem. [ ] Yes [ ] No

Q9: The Problem shouldn't be "too big". [ ] True [ ] False

Q10: Never ask the audience to be physically engaged. [ ] Yes [ ] No

Q11: Why is this slide important to the audience?

Answers:

https://www.ideatogrowth.com/answers-10-slides-to-startup-funding-success/#slide-2-the-problem-slide

Chapter Notes

How Big is the Market Opportunity?

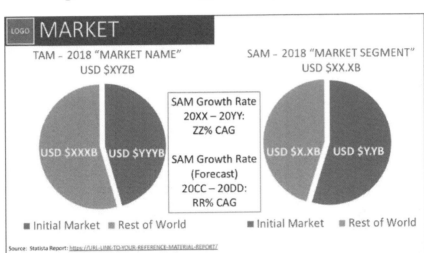

Figure 23 - The Market Slide

The Market Slide — Why Is It Important?

Why do startup investors want to hear about the Market now?

With the Cover Slide, the entrepreneur introduced the startup, themselves and answered the first unspoken startup investor question **Who are you and why am I spending time with you?** (Slide 1).

The startup investors second thought was **What is the Big, Hairy Problem this Startup has Targeted?** (Slide 2)

Now the mind of the startup investor asks, **Big Problem, but how big is the Market which has this Problem?** (Slide 3)

Remember, earlier I commented it is rare for small markets to be of interest to startup investors. Startup investors prefer to invest in USD 1B+ market sizes. The startup investors big payday happens when an acquirer pays 10x to 50x of what the startup investor invested. It is rare for products and services with small markets to provide high rates of return to startup investors. Small markets equate to great difficulty in an entrepreneur discovery of startup investment.

For example, imagine the Problem the startup will address is a disease of 1000 people worldwide contract and die from each year. Therefore, the Total Available Market (TAM) is 1000 customers.

Remember I said startup investors want to invest in USD 1B+ value companies? Even if this imaginary startup was able to find a large company to pay ten times (10X) annual sales valuation (unlikely) to acquire them later, the math indicates the startup needs to reach USD 100M in annual sales.

Even if the Serviceable Addressable Market (SAM) is 100% of the TAM, the math indicates that each of the 1000 customers would have to pay USD 100K per year for the miracle drug.

Remember, the startup will not get 100% of the SAM. Startup investors will often assume the startup will (best-case) get 5% to 10% of the SAM in the first few years, so the smaller the Market size, the lower the potential Revenue and Valuation.

Few startup investors, except one with a family member with this rare disease, will invest in a startup which seeks a cure. Many orphan diseases do not get investments for this reason.

However, say the entrepreneur has developed a universal Takata automotive airbag replacement which costs USD 10 to manufacture.

With the millions of cars worldwide which need to replace defective Takata airbags, the entrepreneur has an investable startup. The Takata startup itself might buy your startup to help save its own business.

The entrepreneur may need to spend cash to buy a report or two to be able to confirm the Market information. I recommend you pay the money for any critical reports. Now is not the time to skimp.

However, before you do spend money to buy a report, check the local library for a copy of the Report(s).

Reach out to the startup who authored the report. Tell the report owners you are an early-stage startup and would appreciate a free copy of the report. If no free copy is available, ask if the firm can share the handful of essential pages needed. A good chance exists that a startup investor interested in the entrepreneur's startup will buy a copy of the report as part of the Due Diligence process. Be creative in your attempt to get a free copy of a report. However, always be honest.

What if the Market SAM is less than USD 1B?

As the entrepreneur digs into the size of the market, they may discover the Market is too small to attract funds. Remember, too small of a market to interest startup investors is one in which the TAM or SAM is below USD 1B.

If the Market analysis falls into this lower end of the investment spectrum, the entrepreneur has three choices.

First, change the product to address a broader Market. Many refer to this choice as a Pivot. However, sometimes a Pivot to a broader market is impossible.

Second, move forward with the first product, accept the startup is a Lifestyle Business. Lifestyle businesses are ones who make a nice income for the startup team but generates too little cash to get an investment other than from Friends and Family.

Lifestyle businesses are unwise investments by startup investors as they will not see the 10X to 50X return on invested capital desired.

Third, the entrepreneur can find a new entrepreneurial idea. Knowing when to pull-the-plug on a specific startup idea is the sign of an experienced entrepreneur and business person.

Pulling the plug on any entrepreneurial adventure is a painful process. Therefore, I recommend the entrepreneur build the Investor Pitch Deck early in the IDEA Stage. The earlier the entrepreneur makes the Investor Pitch Deck, the sooner they will discover the strength of the startup idea.

The Pitch Deck will reveal weaknesses in the business early when the smallest amount of time, capital, and emotional attachment has occurred. The longer the entrepreneur waits to pull the plug, the more critical resources they have spent. The loss of these vital resources means less of each are available to the entrepreneurs next idea.

Time to learn about the Market startup Story content.

The Market Slide - The Startup Story Content

First, write down the critical oral points the startup investor should want to hear when the entrepreneur describes the Market.

What investor questions should the verbal Story answer?

- Document the growth rate of the Market.
- Document the TAM size of the Global Market versus the Local Market.
- Document the SAM size of the Global Market versus the Local Market.
- Document the SAM Growth rate for the last five years, then the forecast for the next five years.
- Document the URL reference to the source data.

Now let us discuss how to Craft and Deliver the Market startup Story.

The Market Slide — Craft the Startup Story

Allow me to provide one example of the Market Slide oral startup pitch which would work well.

The Medical Device Market in 2017 had a Global Total Available Market of USD 289B, with the USA represents USD 177B of the total. The Global Served Available Market of the Product space is USD 3.1B of the total, with USD 1.7B in the USA. The Statista Report estimates the Global SAM, which grew 17% from 2012 through 2017. The forecasted growth is to increase by 23% between 2018 and 2023. These financial numbers show the choice to market the startup solution is an excellent idea.

The entrepreneur has talked about the TAM, the SAM and the critical market numbers which show rapid growth in this market. These are the only topics you need to discuss now.

Now it is time to discuss how to create the Market Slide.

The Market Slide - Create the Slide

In many Investor Pitch Decks, the entrepreneur misses the mark with the Market Slide.

What investor questions should the slide answer?

- Include the slide title *Market*
- Document the growth rate of the Market.
- Document the TAM size of the Global Market versus the Local Market
- Document the SAM size of the Global Market versus the Local Market
- Document the SAM Growth rate for the last five years, then the forecast for the next five years
- Document the URL reference to the source data

So many entrepreneurs I have listened to have said the product targets a USD 100B Market.

However, the entrepreneur does not share in the Investor Pitch Deck the reference source for the claimed USD 100B market.

The entrepreneur has created a huge credibility gap with the startup investor. If you fall into this trap, it is game over time. Pack up your computer bag or briefcase and go home.

Allow me to show an example that I see quite often of how not to construct a Market Slide.

The next slide has several issues.

First, there is too much text. The startup investor will be reading and not listen to the pitch.

Second, the decision to use overlapping circles to represent market sizes was a poor decision. It is non-standard and hard to figure out.

Third, the content does not state what the product is and what the specific market space it.

Fourth, there is no URL to the reference source materials. Did the startup CEO dream the numbers up?

This Market Slide is a total fail.

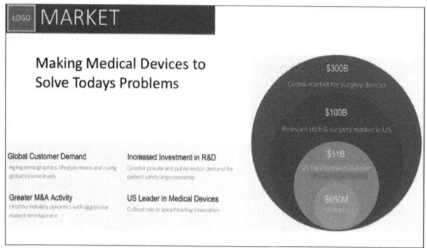

Figure 24 - Market Slide - Bad Example

Now it is time to speak to the right way to construct the Market Slide.

Earlier in the Best Practices chapter, I mentioned the importance of the inclusion of a URL link to the reference on a slide whenever the entrepreneur refers to a third-party source of data. Specifically, the Market Slide was a slide I stated you should have the URL for the Market source reference at both the bottom of the slide and orally referenced in the startup pitch.

Often the entrepreneur may be able to find two to five sources of third-party reports on the Total Available Market (TAM) for the product. The more sources the entrepreneur can discover and refer to regarding the Market size, the more comfortable a startup investor will be with the numbers the entrepreneur presents.

However, while the TAM is a significant number, the SAM is the more important number to the startup investor. Let me explain with another example.

In 2017 the Global Medical Device market was worth an estimated USD 389B. However, the USA part of the Market was USD 177B (Source: Statista Report)

https://www.statista.com/statistics/248676/projected-size-of-the-us-medical-device-industry/

Assume the product is a portable electronic blood pressure measurement device. You dig through the report and find in 2017 USD 3.1B worldwide, and the USA part is USD 1.7B.

Many entrepreneurs would state that the Market size of USD 389B. Such a statement the entrepreneurs would be a lie. The startup would know this, and they will tune out realizing the entrepreneur is at best a novice and at worst a liar.

What is the best method to show a startup investor the Market information? If you remember, back in the Best Practices chapter I told you the Market Slide was a perfect slide to use one to two Pie Charts.

Why two pie charts?

The first pie chart shows the TAM/SAM of the global market.

The second pie chart shows the TAM/SAM for the local market.

The entrepreneur also needs to answer the question about the direction of the market (up or down). Text and numbers answer this question.

Allow me to use one example. Assume the source data reports showed the SAM had grown 17% per year while in the last five years. However, the report estimates the SAM will accelerate to 23% per year for the next five years. These are two crucial numbers the entrepreneur should include in the Market Story. One can present these number as follows:

SAM Growth Rate 2012 - 2017: 17% CAG

SAM Growth Rate 2018 - 2023: 23% CAG (Forecast)

This Market Slide would look like the example shown next.

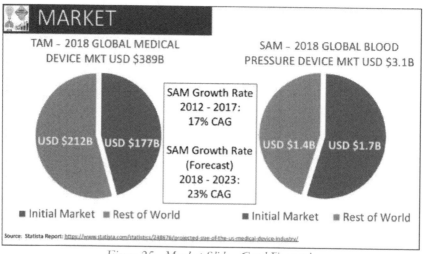

Figure 25 - Market Slide - Good Example

The TAM and the SAM displayed in this manner tells the startup investor several crucial facts.

First, these SAM numbers show how big the product Market is global versus the local market. The difference between the global and regional market sizes are essential to startup investors and entrepreneurs. For many products, the global market is a more significant percentage of the market than the local market.

Second, the SAM and TAM pie charts show to the startup investor the entrepreneur is a global thinker. So many entrepreneurs ignore the global market for the startup product. As the entrepreneur, if this is your thought process, change your thought process before you present to startup investors. Startup investors want entrepreneurial leaders who can Think Global, and Act (Initially) Local. You want the startup investor not to think ***Great product idea. Unfortunately, within a year, the startup leadership will need replacement.***

Third, this content sets the expectation the entrepreneur will be ready to discuss how the startup will go global. Today, even Mom and Pop retail outlets should have a focus on global sales.

Let me provide an example of my Global mindset I put into action a few years ago.

I built my first 25 game applications for the Apple AppStore in 2013. I launched each of the 25 games in all 25 languages on the same day I began to sell the English game versions.

I used Google Translate to translate the text in each game to all 25 languages. My game buyers were able to read the text in their native language and understand how to play each of my games.

My contacts at Apple told me I was one of a handful of developers to have translated their app into all supported languages.

I sold my games on a global scale on day one on the AppStore.

My games attract a worldwide organic group of customers. At my last check, less than 18% of my game players are USA English speakers. So 82% of my revenues come from outside the USA.

As an entrepreneur, do you use a similar thought process?

Now it is time to discuss the Market Backup Slides.

The Market Slide - Backup Slides

The Market Slide backup slides should include:

- URL(s) to any related numbers you shared

- Year-by-Year details of the SAM and TAM by Market

- If available, SAM and TAM by country (state)

Remember, the goal of the Market slide is to show the startup product has both local and global markets and to show the entrepreneur is both a local and global thinker.

The Market Slide - Construction Checklist

Remember these crucial points about the Market Slide startup Story.

- ☐ Use a Master Template
- ☐ Title: MARKET
- ☐ Target USD 1B+ Market SAM Size
- ☐ TAM and SAM
- ☐ Speak to Local and Global Market size
- ☐ Two Pie Charts - No Tables
- ☐ Include links to crucial Reference material
- ☐ Last 3-5 years Actuals
- ☐ Next 3-5 years Forecast
- ☐ All text is LEGIBLE from 100 Feet (~33 Meters)
- ☐ Bold Colors (no pastels or light colors)
- ☐ Have backup slides with added Market details

You can download the Complete Investor Pitch Deck Checklist - *100% FREE* - Click the link below while connected to WiFi.

https://www.ideatogrowth.com/contact-free-download-investor-pitch-deck-checklist

The Market Slide - Executive Summary

The Market Slide Story and Slide include the below info.

- Use of a Master template (Slide)

- *MARKET* for the slide title (Slide)

- A pie chart of the TAM size of the Global Market versus the Local Market (Slide)

- A pie chart of the SAM size of the Global Market versus the Local Market (Slide)

- The financial numbers which show the SAM Growth rate for the last five years (Slide & Story)

- The financial numbers which show the SAM Growth rate forecast for the next five years (Slide & Story)

- Document the URL reference to the source data (Slide)

- Deliver the Market Story in 18-30 seconds (Story)

- Minimize Text - Use Images to Tell the startup Story (Slide)

- The text is Legible from 100 Feet (33 Meters) (Slide)

- Bold Colors (no pastels or light colors) (Slide)

In the next chapter, I will speak about the fourth part of the startup Story — The Solution Slide.

Chapter Quiz

Q1: The slide title should be: Target Customers [ ] Yes [ ] No

Q2: Why is this slide "Important" to the audience?

Q3: What is SAM short for?

Q4: What is TAM short for?

Q5: What is the smallest SAM needed for the largest investor interest?

Q6: Can TAM be smaller than SAM? [ ] Yes [ ] No

Q7: Show only a 1-year SAM/TAM forecast. [ ] Yes [ ] No

Q8: Use respected 3rd party SAM/TAM data. [ ] Yes [ ] No

Q9: Show the URL to data source only on backup slide [ ] Yes [ ] No

Q10: Always use a table filled with relevant SAM/TAM numbers for the Market slide. [ ] Yes [ ] No

Q11: Use a font size no larger than 8 points. [ ] Yes [ ] No

Q12: If you have multiple sources of SAM/TAM data always use the one with the largest numbers regardless of reputation. [ ] Yes [ ] No

Q13: The SAM/TAM data should only be based on your local/regional markets. [ ] Yes [ ] No

Q14: A shrinking SAM/TAM is OK with investors if the market is over $1B in SAM/TAM. [ ] Yes [ ] No

Answers:

https://www.ideatogrowth.com/answers-10-slides-to-startup-funding-success/#slide-3-the-market-slide

Chapter Notes

Our Awesome Solution (Product / Service)

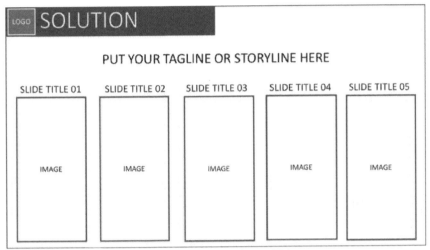

Figure 26 - The Solution Slide

The Solution Slide — Why Is It Important?

Why do startup investors want to hear about the Solution now?

With the Cover Slide, the entrepreneur introduced the startup, themselves and answered the first unspoken startup investor question *Who are you and why am I spending time with you?* (Slide 1).

The startup investors second thought was *What is the Big, Hairy Problem this Startup has Targeted?* (Slide 2)

Next, the startup investors third thought was *Big Problem, but how big is the Market for this Problem?* (Slide 3)

Now the mind of the startup investor asks, *What is the startup Solution for the Market?* (Slide 4)

The Solution startup Story the entrepreneur shares must rock the startup investor. Preferably, the Solution must bring the thought of **Wow!** to the mind of the startup investor. The Solution should be simple for the startup investor to understand the basic workings of, even for complex solutions.

Is the Solution a Durable Good Product?

What do I mean by a durable good product? Typically, a durable good product is a product you sell once to a consumer in a year or more. A toaster is an example of a durable good product. Television is an example of a durable good product. Both items may sell to the same customer more than once in the customers lifetime, but durable good products are not typical products a startup has repeat customer purchases on a month-to-month basis.

Hard-good product solutions are products most consumers and businesses buy. Startup investors often like to invest in startups which make a durable good product because the Product Solution is a physical product solution and not a software product solution. Some startup investors prefer entrepreneurial solutions they can touch versus solutions which are little more than a bunch of electrons.

However, durable good solutions have a significant weakness. For a startup to keep ongoing monthly revenue, they must always find new customers. Current customers generate revenue only if they need to replace the product. For many durable good products, repeat sales are a low single-digit percentage of every month-to-month sales.

Multiple studies have shown it is easier to get repeat sales from a happy current customer than it is to find a new customer to buy your product.

Is the Solution a Consumable Good Product?

What do I mean by consumable good product? Typically, a consumable good product is a product sold on a short-term repeated basis to a customer. An auto insurance policy is an example of a consumable good product. A health club membership is an example of a consumable good product. Both items sell to the same customer via a month-to-month subscription rate, paid monthly, quarterly, semi-annually, or annually.

Startup investors like consumable good solutions because every new customer is an ever-growing monthly, quarterly, semi-annual, and annual revenue stream.

Soft-good solutions often have more stickiness than many durable good products. What do I mean by *stickiness*? *Stickiness* is the likelihood a buyer will buy the product week after week or month after month when there is limited incentive to change.

Is the Solution a Durable and Consumable Product?

If the entrepreneur sells a machine which converts USD 2 wine into wine which tastes like USD 20 wine, the solution is a durable good Product.

A consumable good example would be a monthly software subscription to a software application which educates the customer on the best wines to buy capable of transformation into wines which taste like USD.

If the entrepreneur combines the wine hardware with the software subscription, the entrepreneur has mixed the best of durable good and consumable good product into a superior product solution.

Great durable good products have an associated consumable good part. A joint Solution will attract more startup investor interest (think Apple iPhone with all the available Paid Services one can buy).

Time to learn about the Solution startup Story content.

The Solution Slide - The Startup Story Content

First, write down the critical oral points the startup investor should want to hear when the entrepreneur describes the Solution.

What investor questions should the verbal Story answer?

- Hard-good Solution - Describe the Product
- Consumable Good Solution - Use screenshots to show the critical usage steps and describe the ease of use
- Combo Solution - List the SaaS features
- List Solutions to Problem Slide items

Now let us discuss how to Craft and Deliver the Solution startup Story.

The Solution Slide — Craft the Startup Story

Think back to the Problem Slide. The Solution Slide startup Story should address every Problem point. Also, if a startup investor asks a question the entrepreneur must answer their question.

If the startup has a physical product, avoid the physical display of the product at this point in the presentation. Remember, as the entrepreneur you are on the clock. Save a product demo for a later time. If you defer the product demo, this will whet the appetite of the startup investor, which should be a goal of the entrepreneur.

Avoid consumable good product demos. A software demo is a sure-fire recipe for failure. Networks fail. Computers will freeze. A software demo will always blow the time budget.

Allow me to provide one example of the Solution Slide oral startup pitch which would work well.

I will use one of the companies I coached is a Tampa Bay WaVE Accelerator company. The startup is known as Harness.

Harness created a phone application to enable effortless consumer donations to favorite charities. Install the mobile app on the iPhone or Android Phone. Enter your often-used credit or debit card. You are now set up to donate to your favorite charity.

Every time you buy an item with your registered credit card, the credit card startup notifies the application of the amount, and the app records the difference in pennies between the purchase amount and the next rounded up dollar amount.

At the end of the billing period, the app adds together all these round-up penny differences of each of the transactions made for the month and sends a single charge to your credit card.

The total monthly donation transfers to the charities bank account electronically, minus a small transaction fee paid to Harness. You get a by month, by quarter, and an annual Donation Report you can use when you file your taxes.

Each charity can include a short video to show the typical use of donations. Think of the video as feel-good feedback to contributors.

Additionally, a charity can white-label the Harness product, so the app has a custom look-and-feel tied to the charity. The Ronald McDonald House was an early adopter of the Harness white-label product.

Now with the knowledge of the background on the Harness product, what might the oral startup pitch for the Solution Slide be?

Allow me to introduce Harness — Turn Casual Supporters into Lifetime Donors. Earlier, I mentioned the many challenges of the typical consumer who wants to donate to a favorite Charity. Harness solves all those challenges with elegance and with cost-effectiveness.

The Harness app takes every registered credit or debit card transaction and records the difference between the charged amount and the next roundup dollar amount. The Harness app saves these round-up differences while in the month and then records the total as a single charge to your credit or debit card. You can set a maximum dollar amount by-the-month transaction to limit donations to a set budget.

If you are at an event for the charity or have a few extra dollars you want to donate from time to time, the Harness app lets you do so with a click or two.

You can also view a charity supplied video which shows the uses of a charitable donation.

Each month you can go into the app to view a report of all the previous donations. Each year you will see a summary of all the contributions for the year. A donation summary eases the completion of the charitable donations section of your tax form.

For the charities themselves, Harness offers a white-label choice of the product. A white-label version of the Harness product allows each charity to customize the app and so donations to the charity is effortless. The Ronald McDonald House is one of the early adopters of the HarnessApp white-label program and is happy with its success to date.

Harness - Turn Casual Supporters into Lifetime Donors!

Impressed with the oral part of the startup pitch? The startup investors will be impressed with your version of your startup Story when you think about the Harness example.

The company Harness has fundraised more than USD 1.2M.

Now it is time to discuss how to create the Solution Slide.

The Solution Slide — Create the Slide

What investor questions should the slide answer?

- Include the slide title **Solution**.

- Show images related to the product in use.

Now the entrepreneur has the startup Story mapped out they can put the slide together with ease.

Before we review how to make the Solution Slide the right way, let us look at how not to make a Solution Slide.

In the example below, the entrepreneur has shown a sketch of their breakthrough product, a Teleportation machine. So why is this the wrong way to show the Solution?

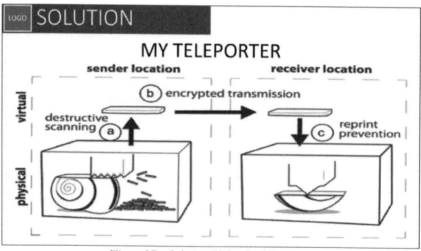

Figure 27 - Solution Slide - Bad Example

First, the slide shows a sketch of the product, not the actual product. Presenting the Solution in this manner is telling the startup investor that the product is still in the IDEA Stage and there is not an

MVP. If the product existed, the entrepreneur would show an actual picture of the Teleportation product.

Now let us make a Solution Slide using the recommended method. Go back and examine the example Harness oral pitch I wrote. You want to have supported content on the slide for each critical point.

Remember the tagline? Harness — Turn Casual Supporters into Lifetime Donors. Create a text box at the top of the slide.

Harness uses the Round-Up method, so a donation to your favorite charities is effortless. Take a screenshot indicative of this part of the process and put a label above the image on the slide.

The capability of the application to allow donation at an event or whenever the donor had a few extra dollars was important. Take a screenshot indicative of this part of the process and put a label above the image on the slide.

Each charity supplied a video which showcases the typical uses of donations. Take a screenshot indicative of this part of the process and put a label above the image on the slide.

The next point covered how the application user could view month-to-month and annual donation amounts in a report inside the app for tax purposes. Take a screenshot indicative of this part of the process and put a label above the image on the slide.

Lastly, I mentioned how Ronald McDonald was an early adopter of the Harness white label program. Take a screenshot indicative of this part of the process and put a label above the image on the slide.

If you do all I ascribed to above, the Solution Slide should look like the next image.

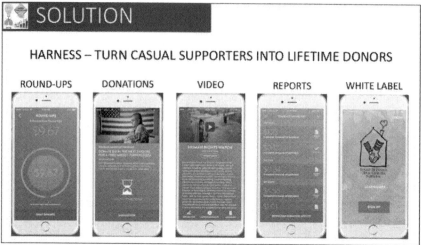

Figure 28 - Solution Slide - Good Example

The startup tagline is front and center. The five product feature sets have a visual example the entrepreneur can refer to as they tell the startup Solution Story.

Now it is time to discuss the Solution Backup Slides.

The Solution Slide - Backup Slides

The Solution Slide backup slides should include:

- More detailed Product images

- A slide which details the Product Solution for each issue listed on Problem slide and other unlisted Problems

Remember, the goal of the Solution slide is to show off the killer Solution the startup has created.

The Solution Slide - Construction Checklist

Remember these crucial points about the Solution Slide startup Story.

- ☐ Use a Master Template
- ☐ Title: SOLUTION
- ☐ Use Simple Title on each Image
- ☐ Use one or a series of images to display your product
- ☐ If multiple images, use a 1-2-word title above or below each
- ☐ Ideally, images should clearly relate back to the Problem
- ☐ Minimize Text - Use Images to Tell the startup Story
- ☐ The text is Legible from 100 Feet (33 Meters)
- ☐ Bold Colors (no pastels or light colors)
- ☐ Have backup slides with added product details

You can download the Complete Investor Pitch Deck Checklist - **100% FREE** - Click the link below while connected to WiFi.

https://www.ideatogrowth.com/contact-free-download-investor-pitch-deck-checklist

The Solution Slide - Executive Summary

The Solution Slide Story and Slide include the below info.

- Use of a Master template (Slide)

- *SOLUTION* for the slide title (Slide)

- Image(s) of the Solution (Slide & Story)

- The title above or on each Image (Slide)

- Deliver the Solution Story in 18-30 seconds (Story)

- Minimize Text - Use Images to Tell the startup Story (Slide)

- The text is Legible from 100 Feet (33 Meters) (Slide)

- Bold Colors (no pastels or light colors) (Slide)

In the next chapter, I will speak about the fifth part of the startup Story — The Traction Slide.

Also, be sure to check out the Resources page for helpful downloads! There is also a link to save you dozens of hours building your own Investor Pitch Deck Slide template. For book buyers I include a discount code that will save you $$$.

Click RESOURCES to jump to the download page now.

Chapter Quiz

Q1: The slide title should be "Our Product". [ ] Yes [ ] No

Q2: The Solution "must" always be the lowest priced. [ ] Yes [ ] No

Q3: The Solution should be a bit mysterious and vague. [ ] Yes [ ] No

Q4: If the Solution is a physical product, now is the time to show it and pass it around the audience. [ ] Yes [ ] No

Q5: If the Solution is a SaaS product, now is the time to do a website or app demo. [ ] Yes [ ] No

Q6: The Solution slide should take less time than any other slide. [ ] Yes [ ] No

Q7: Investors often prefer investments that have both a hardware and SaaS part over one or the other only. [ ] Yes [ ] No

Q8: A Hardware-based company is more investable that a SaaS company. [ ] Yes [ ] No

Q9: Ideally, the Solution is unique. [ ] Yes [ ] No

Q10: The Solution must have a patent to get investment. [ ] Yes [ ] No

Answers:

https://www.ideatogrowth.com/answers-10-slides-to-startup-funding-success/#slide-4-the-solution-slide

Chapter Notes

_____

_____

_____

_____

_____

_____

_____

_____

_____

_____

_____

_____

_____

_____

_____

_____

_____

Is Anyone Buying the MVP?

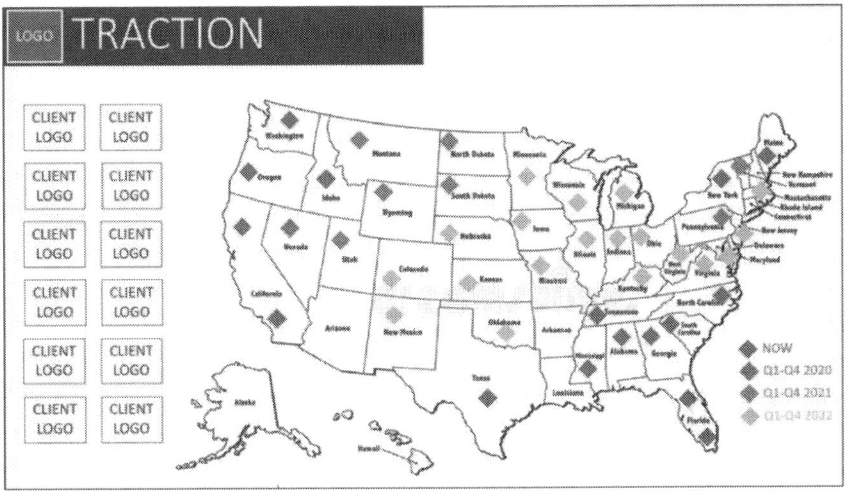

Figure 29 - The Traction Slide

The Traction Slide — Why Is It Important?

Why do startup investors want to hear about the Traction now?

With the Cover Slide, the entrepreneur introduced the startup, themselves and answered the first unspoken startup investor question *Who are you and why am I spending time with you?* (Slide 1).

The startup investors second thought was *What is the Big, Hairy Problem this Startup has Targeted?* (Slide 2)

Next, the startup investors third thought was *Big Problem, but how big is the Market for this Problem?* (Slide 3)

The startup investors fourth thought was *What is the startup Solution for this Market?* (Slide 4)

Now the mind of the startup investor asks, ***Great Solution. How much Market Traction does the startup have?*** (Slide 5)

My Startup is pre-MVP

If the startup is pre-MVP, I urge against such early fundraising. The exception is if the Solution takes significant funds to build an MVP.

If the startup is pre-MVP, I also recommend against the use of funds from Friends and Family. Regardless of what most Friends and Family would say, the loss of all their investment (as most startups at this stage fail) will have a negative impact on the relationship with the entrepreneur.

Reach out to startup investors and fundraise if the startup idea has high startup costs. As I stated earlier, many great ideas need funds to create an MVP. Entrepreneurs should not delay the start of a startup because startup investors will end up with majority ownership. Great startup investors realize that entrepreneurs must end up with enough ownership of the startup for the entrepreneur to stay with the company.

If the entrepreneur can find pre-MVP startup investors, they will demand a higher percentage of startup ownership because of the higher investment risk.

I recommend the entrepreneur bootstrap the startup until an MVP exists to show to startup investors.

My Startup is pre-Revenue

What if the startup is in the pre-Revenue stage?

In most cases, this means the entrepreneur is presenting too early for many startup investors. Exceptions do exist. Angel investors and pre-Revenue venture capital funds will invest in new markets, emerging markets, and markets in which they have experience.

If the entrepreneur has experience and a unique solution to a Problem in an investable space, there is a good chance the entrepreneur can fundraise.

The loss of an entrepreneurs ownership with an early investment is higher than if the entrepreneur can delay a fundraiser until after making product sales to enough customers. Proving that the product has customers willing to pay the product prices that the entrepreneur will later discuss in the Financials Slide is essential to many investors.

Time to learn about the Traction startup Story content.

The Traction Slide - The Startup Story Content

First, write down the critical oral points the startup investor should want to hear when the entrepreneur describes the Traction.

- Who are the Customers?
- Where are the Customers found?
- What is the Customer acquisition plan by region?
- What is the Customer acquisition plan? (12m - 24m - 36m)

Startup traction is different from startup revenues. I discuss startup revenues later in the Financial Slide.

The Traction part of the startup Story is all about Customers. The timeframe you should speak to should cover the current customers and the customer acquisition plan for the next 8-12 calendar quarters

What investor questions should the verbal Story answer?

- Names of crucial Customers are in product evaluation
- Names of essential Customers have placed purchase orders
- Names of critical Customers who have made purchases
- Essential target Customer names

Now let us discuss how to Craft and Deliver the Traction startup Story.

The Traction Slide — Craft the Startup Story

Allow me to provide one example of the Traction Slide oral startup pitch which would work well.

I will use one of my business coach clients, MyArea Network. MyArea Network is a hybrid of an Advertising and Market Development startup headquartered in Tampa, FL.

Next, I would like to speak to MyArea Network Customer Traction.

Our current clients include companies such as Hungry Howie, New York Yankees, Hard Rock Casino, Marriott, AAA, Samuel Adams, Beef Brady, and Captain Morgan, to name a few.

MyArea Network sells online search advertising in 8 Active markets. This slide shows the next 15 Growth markets and the following 35 Build markets. Customers can sign up in more than 100 Live markets. These 100+ markets all generate traffic and growth. In 2018, the goal is to be Active in 10 added markets outside of Florida, more than doubles the number of Active marketplaces.

Here are some of the top opportunities for 2018. Hungry Howie for example, which started as a USD 500 a month client is now a six-figure client with them to become a seven-figure client as the marketing across all Florida stores rolls out.

While customer Traction focus has been in Florida, from the map one can see the next Ramp-Up markets will include Texas, Colorado, Maryland, Chicago, California, and Washington. Many of these locations are states where current Florida customers have operations.

MyArea Network has also identified Development Markets which include Georgia, South Carolina, North Carolina, Virginia, and several others as shown. This Customer Traction plan will enable strong fiscal growth while in the next 18 months.

Notable example story and one which will get the entrepreneur to ask for a Second-Date!

Now it is time to discuss how to create the Traction Slide.

The Traction Slide — Create the Slide

What investor questions should the slide answer?

- Who are the Customers? (Logos)

- Where are the Customers found? (Map)

- What is the Customer acquisition plan by region? (Map)

- What is the Customer acquisition plan? (12m - 24m - 36m) (Map)

The Traction Slide is all about how much Traction the startup has with Customers. There is a temptation to title this slide **Customers**. I recommend the entrepreneur avoid the use of **Customers** as the title for this slide.

A slide with the title **Traction** speaks with more strength to a startup investor. **Traction** is a more powerful topic title than the topic inferred by the title **Customers**.

Before I show you a good Traction Slide example, allow me to share a common Traction Slide example that I do not recommend.

In the example slide below you see that the entrepreneur has used the title Customers and not Traction. The entrepreneur has created a simple list of customers. This slide provides no critical details. Where are the customers located? How many customer locations are selling the product? What is the product rollout plan over the next 12 months? The following 24 months? Also, the entrepreneur used the textual names and not the logos, so the entrepreneur is reading the slide to the startup investor. Yikes!

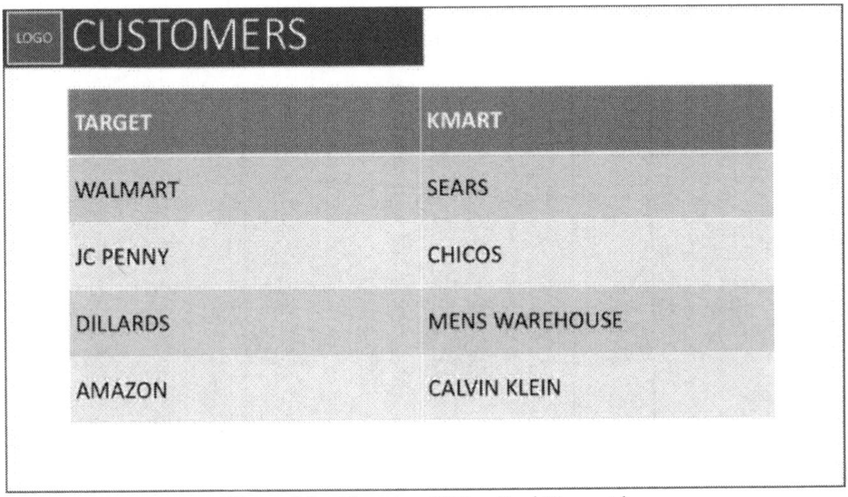

LOGO CUSTOMERS

TARGET	KMART
WALMART	SEARS
JC PENNY	CHICOS
DILLARDS	MENS WAREHOUSE
AMAZON	CALVIN KLEIN

Figure 30 - Traction Slide - Bad Example

A combination of corporate logos and a regional map outline is a great technique to use for construction of the Traction Slide. I like corporate logos because a corporate image is more straightforward to remember and recognize versus a group of letters. Use of company logos rather than the textual name, the startup investor will not feel like the entrepreneur is reading the words on the slide to them.

I like to include on the Traction Slide a regional map. If the business has its headquarters in the USA, the state outline map of the USA with two-letter state identifiers is an excellent choice.

If the startup has Germany, Spain or another European country headquarters, the map outline might be of greater Europe.

What might an excellent Traction Slide look like for MyArea Network? Examine the next image. What do you see? You see a group of startup logos and a USA map with states outlined.

These are the badges of the first customers who prove the Solutions value. These companies either buy from the startup or are product/service evaluation. If the startup has 50+ customers, list customers with the highest revenue or highest startup investor recognition.

Figure 31 - Traction Slide - Good Example

The top client logos appear on the slide. I chose to spread the logos around the map to cause the startup investors eyes to view the entirety of the slide, rather than focus on a single spot or area.

The startup investor also sees a map outline of the entrepreneur's region of the world where the startup customers are based. Different color-coded flags signify the status of the various regional sales focusses of Active, Ramp-up, Development and Next. These labels have a direct tie to the oral startup Story of the startup pitch.

Now it is time to discuss the Traction Backup Slides.

The Traction Slide - Backup Slides

The Traction Slide backup slides should include:

- A slide on each significant Customer with annual revenue

- A slide of the Customer rollout plan by month for 36 months

- A detailed slide for a rollout plan on financial strategy

- A detailed slide on Customer Acquisition Methods

Remember, the goal of the Traction slide is to highlight the current and planned customer engagement.

The Traction Slide - Construction Checklist

Remember these crucial points about the Traction Slide startup Story.

- ☐ Use a Master Template
- ☐ Title: TRACTION
- ☐ Use Logo for each Client
- ☐ Regional rollout maps are good to use
- ☐ Differentiate between current and future Clients
- ☐ Backup slides with details on the size of each Client, Warm vs. Cold Introductions, and Acquisition method plans
- ☐ All text is Legible from 100 Feet (33 Meters)
- ☐ Bold Colors (no pastels or light colors)

You can download the Complete Investor Pitch Deck Checklist - *100% FREE* - Click the link below while connected to WiFi.

https://www.ideatogrowth.com/contact-free-download-investor-pitch-deck-checklist

The Traction Slide - Executive Summary

The Traction Slide Story and Slide include the below info.

- Use of a Master template (Slide)
- **TRACTION** for the slide title (Slide)
- Who are the Customers? (Logos) (Slide & Story)
- Where are the Customers found? (Map) (Slide & Story)
- Customer acquisition plan by region? (Map) (Slide & Story)
- Customer acquisition plan? (12m - 24m - 36m) (Map) (Slide & Story)
- Which crucial Customers are in product evaluation? (Slide & Story)
- Which crucial Customers have placed purchase orders? (Slide & Story)
- Which crucial Customers have received product deliveries? (Slide & Story)
- Who are the future crucial target Customers? (Slide & Story)
- Deliver the Traction Story in 18-30 seconds (Story)
- Minimize Text - Use Images to Tell the startup Story (Slide)
- The text is Legible from 100 Feet (33 Meters) (Slide)
- Bold Colors (no pastels or light colors) (Slide)

In the next chapter, I will speak about the sixth part of the startup Story — The Competition Slide.

Chapter Quiz

Q1: The slide title should be "Our Sales". [ ] Yes [ ] No

Q2: The easiest time to get investment is "before" you have sales. [ ] Yes [ ] No

Q3: If you have no sales, you should leave the Traction slide out of your pitch deck. [ ] Yes [ ] No

Q4: What four things should the Traction backup slide have?

Q5: Always use customer names and never their logos. [ ] Yes [ ] No

Q6: A regional or world map is a good slide graphic. [ ] Yes [ ] No

Q7: Mix actual with future customers into a single graphic to make your company look like it has more customers. [ ] Yes [ ] No

Q8: A table on this slide is preferable to a graphic. [ ] Yes [ ] No

Q9: If you have many customers, feature the recognizable companies. [ ] Yes [ ] No

Q10: How many seconds should your Traction Story use in a 6-minute overall pitch?

Answers:

https://www.ideatogrowth.com/answers-10-slides-to-startup-funding-success/#slide-5-the-traction-slide

Chapter Notes

_____

_____

_____

_____

_____

_____

_____

_____

_____

_____

_____

_____

_____

_____

_____

_____

_____

Our Startup Company versus the Competition

FEATURE COMPARISON	YOUR LOGO	COMPETITOR LOGO	COMPETITOR LOGO	COMPETITOR LOGO	COMPETITOR LOGO	COMPETITOR LOGO
FEATURE 1	✓	✓	X	✓	X	X
FEATURE 2	✓	X	✓	✓	✓	✓
FEATURE 3	✓	X	✓	X	✓	X
FEATURE 4	✓	✓	X	✓	X	X
FEATURE 5	✓	✓	✓	X	X	X
FEATURE 6	✓	X	X	✓	✓	✓
FEATURE 7	✓	✓	X	X	X	X
FEATURE 8	✓	X	X	X	✓	✓

Figure 32 - The Competition Slide

The Competition Slide — Why Is It Important?

Why do startup investors want to hear about the Competition now?

With the Cover Slide, the entrepreneur introduced the startup, themselves and answered the first unspoken startup investor question *Who are you and why am I spending time with you?* (Slide 1).

The startup investors second thought was *What is the Big, Hairy Problem this Startup has Targeted?* (Slide 2)

Next, the startup investors third thought was *Big Problem, but how big is the Market for this Problem?* (Slide 3)

The startup investors fourth thought was *What is the startup Solution for the Market?* (Slide 4)

Next, the startup investors fifth thought was *Great Solution. How much Market Traction does the startup have?* (Slide 5)

Now the mind of the startup investor asks, *What level of Competition does the Startup face and how does the startup Solution stack up against the Competition?* (Slide 6)

We Have No Competition!

Avoid this mistake I have heard from too many entrepreneurs.

Do not say; *We Have No Competition.*

We Have No Competition is a fatal statement for the entrepreneur if they want to fundraise. To make this statement the entrepreneur has told startup investors they are extremely inexperienced.

Remember this fact. For every Problem, there is some current Solution. Even if the entrepreneur invented Teleportation, there exist competitive Solutions. The automobile, the plane, the bus, your legs, can all get you from point A to point B, albeit with less speed than teleportation.

The startup Solution faces brute force competitive solutions similar to the above. Big corporate competitors and other startups who build their Solutions to target the same problems also exist.

Research the Competition. Find out who the competitors are, both big and small. Learn the market share of each competitor. Find out who has invested in the competitive startups and the total amount of investment in each startup.

Time to learn about the Competition startup Story content.

The Competition Slide - The Startup Story Content

First, write down the critical oral points the startup investor should want to hear when the entrepreneur describes the Competition.

What investor questions should the verbal Story answer?

- Who is each of the competitors? (Logos)
- What is the location of the competitor? (Backup)
- How big is each competitor? (Backup)
- List the crucial product features of the startup solution versus competitive solutions (Table)

The entrepreneur will speak to the critical product attributes which highlight the Problems described in the Problem Slide.

List four to eight crucial startup Product differentiators as compared to the Competitors product. Later when one creates the talking points, focus on the top three to four features and speak as to why those features are essential, unique solutions to customers.

Point out the fact all four to eight crucial product differentiators listed on the Competition Slide are present in the startup product. However, one or more crucial product differentiators are missing on competitor products.

Give each of the crucial four to five features about five seconds each and review why Customers see this as a must-have feature.

Due to time constraints, the entrepreneur will not mention all competitors. However, the entrepreneur must know who each significant competitor is.

Now let us discuss how to Craft and Deliver the Competition startup Story.

The Competition Slide — Craft the Startup Story

Allow me to provide one example of the Competition Slide oral startup pitch which would work well.

Seven crucial features exist which Customers need. The slide shows the startup Solution satisfies all seven, while the closest two Competitors, satisfies two.

One competitor is a three-year-old startup who has fundraised USD 12M. The other competitor is a division of XYZ corporation.

Unlike our competitors, MyArea Network has both an online Customer and Channel portal. The competition requires customers and channel partners to phone the vendor.

Our customers estimate annual savings on these two features alone are more than USD 100K.

Our third crucial feature is a single-click Customer registration, via a free branded iOS and Android app. At one customer, this feature has already increased product registrations by 2X, which has allowed product up-sales of more than USD 100K.

All 17 customers MyArea Network has taken from one of the listed competitors on the strength of the MyArea Network Product Feature set.

Now it is time to discuss how to create the Competition Slide.

The Competition Slide — Create the Slide

What investor questions should the slide answer?

- Include the slide titled **Competition**

- Who is each of the competitors? (Logos)

- List the crucial product features of the startup solution versus competitive solutions (Table)

Before I show you the right way to do the Competition Slide, allow me to explain how not to construct one.

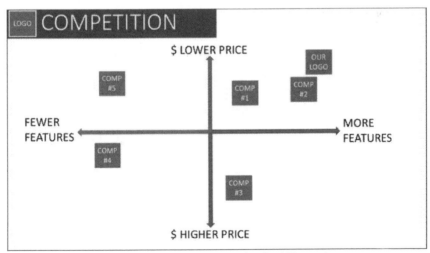

Figure 33 - Competition Slide - Bad Example

ANGEL INVESTORS TO VENTURE CAPITAL
10 SLIDES TO STARTUP FUNDING SUCCESS

This XY slide layout is a conventional technique for separating your startup from the competition. However, to a startup investor, an XY chart lacks critical information. An XY chart can usually only compare two features. The startup investor wants to know differentiation details about your product versus your competition.

The XY slide technique usually is used to show that you have a lower price and more features. *A race to the bottom* often identifies this technique. This slide tells the investor you base your competitiveness on adding more functionality to the product and selling it at a lower price.

That is not often a winning business formula for a startup company or startup investors.

Earlier in the Best Practices chapter, I mentioned the Competition Slide was the perfect slide for the use of a table.

The top of each column has a competitor corporate logo. The first column to the right of the column of critical features is the startup logo. Each column to the right of the startup logo column also begins with the corporate logo of a principal competitor.

The Competitor Slide is where the entrepreneur will highlight the top five to eight crucial differentiators of the startup product. Most of these critical features the competitors hopefully will lack.

The startup column should use bold, green checkmarks associated with each crucial feature. The Competitor has some of the essential features marked with unbolded green checkmarks. Put a red letter *X* or a gray colored dash character where the Competitors lack an essential element.

Examine the next slide I created as an example of how to put together a Competition Slide.

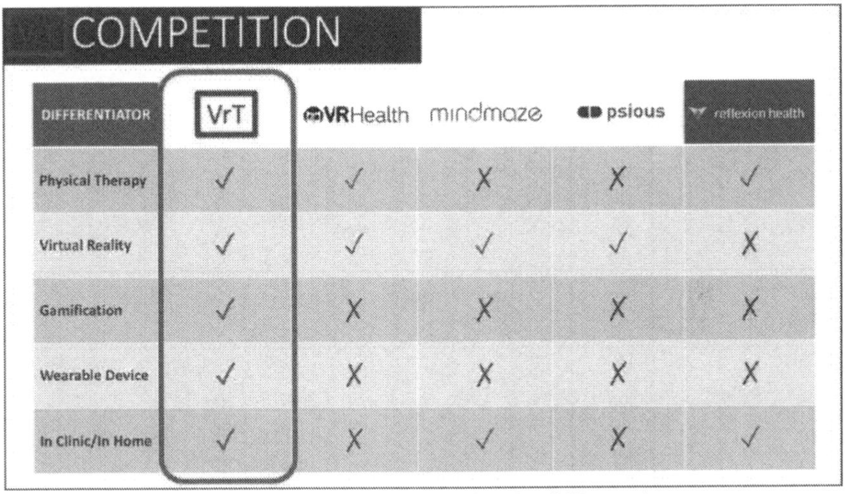

COMPETITION

DIFFERENTIATOR	VrT	VRHealth	mindmaze	psious	reflexion health
Physical Therapy	✓	✓	X	X	✓
Virtual Reality	✓	✓	✓	✓	X
Gamification	✓	X	X	X	X
Wearable Device	✓	X	X	X	X
In Clinic/In Home	✓	X	✓	X	✓

Figure 34 - Competition Slide - Good Example

In this example, VrT has listed four competitors. VrT uses corporate logos at the top of each of the four rightmost columns.

In the leftmost column, VrT has named five of the critical product differentiators. VrT has done competitor research on the essential issues from the Problem Slide and showed these vital issues as essential Product features.

Now it is time to discuss the Competition Backup Slides.

The Competition Slide - Backup Slides

The Competition Slide backup slides should include:

- Who is the competition?

- How big is each competitor?

- Market share for each competitor $>= 5\%$?

- Why do customers buy from each competitor?

- Competitor compelling product?

- Why is each of these critical features important to Customers?

- How difficult is an essential feature to manufacture or duplicate?

- Have the competitors patented any of the crucial features?

- Is any new essential feature you have added patentable?

- Which of the Competitors are startups?

- Who are the startup investors in each startup and how much invested?

- Which competitors are divisions of USD 1B+ companies?

- What stops competitors from the construction of a clone of the startup solution?

- Does the Solution have the traits of a robust startup or is the Solution a Product and not a startup company?

Remember, the goal of the Competition slide is to highlight the critical problems the startup solution brings to the customers unsolved by the competitive product solutions.

The Competition Slide - Construction Checklist

Remember these crucial points about the Competition Slide startup Story.

- ☐ Use a Master Template
- ☐ Title: COMPETITION
- ☐ Single table
- ☐ Five to eight crucial features
- ☐ Four to six critical competitors
- ☐ Current & next 4-8 Quarters Pie Chart (if applicable)
- ☐ All text is LEGIBLE from 100 Feet (33 Meters)
- ☐ Bold Colors (no pastels or light colors)
- ☐ Have backup slides with all Competitors and all Features

You can download the Complete Investor Pitch Deck Checklist - **100% FREE** - Click the link below while connected to WiFi.

https://www.ideatogrowth.com/contact-free-download-investor-pitch-deck-checklist

The Competition Slide - Executive Summary

The Competition Slide Story and Slide include the below info.

First, write down the critical oral points the startup investor should want to hear when the entrepreneur describes the Competition.

- Use of a Master template (Slide)

- ***COMPETITION*** for the slide title (Slide)

- Who is each competitor? (Logos) (Slide & Story)

- What is the location of each competitor? (Backup Slide)

- How big is each competitor? (Backup Slide)

- List the crucial product features of the startup solution versus competitive solutions (Table) (Slide & Story)

- Deliver the Competition Story in 18-30 seconds (Story)

- Minimize Text - Use Images to Tell the startup Story (Slide)

- The text is Legible from 100 Feet (33 Meters) (Slide)

- Bold Colors (no pastels or light colors) (Slide)

In the next chapter, I will speak about the seventh part of the startup Story — The Monetization Slide.

Chapter Quiz

Q1: Only list large, recognizable competitors. [ ] Yes [ ] No

Q2: Include well-funded startups in your list. [ ] Yes [ ] No

Q3: Ignore generic, easy solutions as competition. [ ] Yes [ ] No

Q4: Use a table with green checkmarks, and red/gray "X's" and competitor logos as a best-practice for this slide. [ ] Yes [ ] No

Q5: What should the title of this slide be?

Q6: Include a list of up to 20 key features on this slide. [ ] Yes [ ] No

Q7: Only list features clearly related to the Problem and Solution. [ ] Yes [ ] No

Q8: A listed feature doesn't need to be a customer "must-have". [ ] Yes [ ] No

Q9: Backup slides should include market share details for each competitor listed and all that make up 5% or more market share. [ ] Yes [ ] No

Q10: If you have no competition, you can skip this slide. [ ] Yes [ ] No

Answers:

https://www.ideatogrowth.com/answers-10-slides-to-startup-funding-success/#slide-6-the-competition-slide

Chapter Notes

Revenue Model - Ways You Make Money

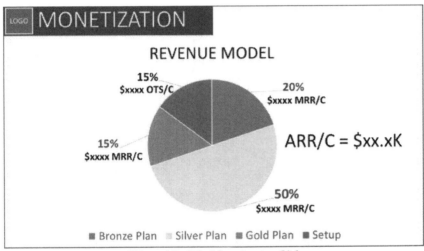

Figure 35 - The Monetization Slide

The Monetization Slide — Why Is It Important?

Why do startup investors want to hear about the Monetization now?

With the Cover Slide, the entrepreneur introduced the startup, themselves and answered the first unspoken startup investor question *Who are you and why am I spending time with you?* (Slide 1).

The startup investors second thought was *What is the Big, Hairy Problem this Startup has Targeted?* (Slide 2)

Next, the startup investors third thought was *Big Problem, but how big is the Market for this Problem?* (Slide 3)

The startup investors fourth thought was *What is the startup Solution for the Market?* (Slide 4)

Next, the startup investors fifth thought was *Great Solution. How much Market Traction does the startup have?* (Slide 5)

The startup investors sixth thought was *What level of Competition does the Startup face and how does the startup Solution stack up against the Competition?* (Slide 6)

Now the mind of the startup investor asks, *What are all the Diverse Ways you Generate Revenue?* (Slide 7)

Time to learn about the Monetization startup Story content.

The Monetization Slide - The Startup Story Content

First, write down the critical oral points the startup investor should want to hear when the entrepreneur describes the Monetization methods the startup is using to generate revenue.

The entrepreneur should speak to all the diverse methods the startup products and services bring in sales.

Does the startup build durable good products?

What investor questions should the verbal Story answer?

- Do you sell direct, through distribution, or both?
- What percentage do you sell direct?
- What percentage do you sell through distribution?
- Is SaaS a part of the Monetization methods?

Does the startup build consumable good products? Be able to break down the difference in revenue streams.

What investor questions should the verbal Story answer?

- Is there a Bronze, Silver, and Gold (or similar) SaaS plans?
- What percentage of revenue does each revenue stream bring in annually?
- Is there a One-Time Setup charge?
- Are there up-sales, down-sales, other revenue generation methods? What % of total revenue to each represent?

Now let us discuss how to Craft and Deliver the Monetization startup Story.

The Monetization Slide — Craft the Startup Story

Allow me to provide one example of the Monetization Slide oral startup pitch which would work well.

GNRB is a Software-as-a-Service (SaaS) business. GNRB generates revenue by via a One-time Setup Fee and a Monthly Service Fee.

GNRB Monthly Recurring Revenue (MRR) price for Bronze, Silver, and Gold packages are USD 500, USD 1000 and USD 1500 respectively.

Per Client Setup fees are USD 495, USD 995 and USD 1995, respectively.

Distribution of GNRB Annual Recurring Revenue sales for each of the three packages are 23%, 50%, and 15%, respectively.

GNRB Annual One-Time Setup Fees per Customer has an ARR of 12% and average annual revenue of USD 1200.

GNRB Annual Recurring Revenue per Customer is USD 13.2K.

GNRB estimate average Customer Lifetime Value (CLV / CLTV) to be 36 months and USD 39.6K.

Wow. The startup has an impressive, high ASP SaaS business. The startup investor has the critical metrics on how the startup generates revenue.

Now it is time to discuss how to create the Monetization Slide.

The Monetization Slide — Create the Slide

Now you have the startup Story mapped out, the assembly of the slide is straightforward.

Go back and examine each paragraph I have written. You want to have supported content on the slide for each crucial point.

Software-as-a-Service Startup Company Slide

Let us create an example of a SaaS startup.

What investor questions should the slide answer?

The imaginary SaaS startup has four revenue streams:

- Bronze Plan
- Silver Plan
- Gold Plan
- One-Time Setup

The respective ARR percentage for each revenue piece is 23%, 50%, 15%, and 12%, respectively.

The respective MRR for each revenue piece is USD 500/C, USD 1000/C, USD 1500/C, and USD 1200/C, respectively.

The Monetization Slide should look like the example I show next.

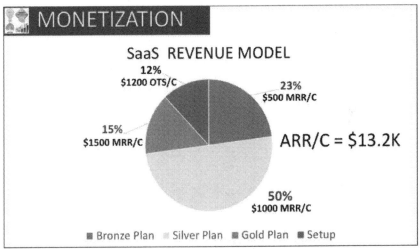

Figure 36 - SaaS Startup Revenue Model

The slide above is a clean pie chart with limited text which supports the entrepreneur's oral startup Story.

Hardware Startup Company Slide

Next, let us use a hardware startup example.

What investor questions should the slide answer?

The imaginary hardware startup has four revenue streams:

- iPhone Hardware Product Sales

- Mac Hardware Product Sales

- iPad Hardware Sale

- iPod Hardware Sales

The 2018 revenue model would break down as 72% to iPhone, 11% to Mac, 10% to iPad and 8% to iPod.

The Monetization Slide should look like what I show next.

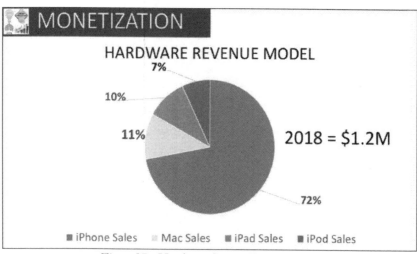

Figure 37 - Hardware Startup Revenue Model

The slide above is a clean pie chart with limited text which supports the entrepreneur's oral startup Story.

Hardware with SaaS Startup Company Slide

Let us create an example of a startup who manufactures a hardware product includes a SaaS feature with every sale.

What investor questions should the slide answer?

The imaginary Hardware plus SaaS startup has six revenue streams:

- Direct Hardware Product Sale
- Distribution Hardware Product Sale
- SaaS Bronze Plan
- SaaS Silver Plan
- SaaS Gold Plan
- SaaS One-Time Setup

The hardware business is expected to generate 73% direct sales and 27% through distribution.

The respective ARR percentage for each revenue piece is 23%, 50%, 15%, and 12%, respectively.

The respective MRR for each revenue piece is USD 500/C, USD 1000/C, USD 1500/C, and USD 1200/C, respectively.

The Monetization Slide should look like the example I show next.

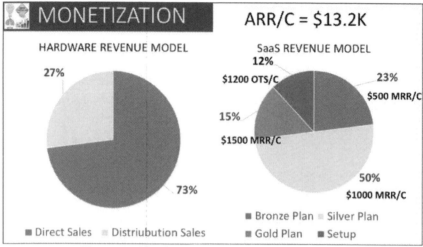

Figure 38 - Hardware + SaaS Startup Revenue Model

This slide shows two pie charts. The first pie chart shows the hardware monetization plan. The second pie chart shows the SaaS monetization plan. The contents of these two pie charts are what the entrepreneur will reference while they deliver the startup pitch.

Now it is time to discuss the Monetization Backup Slides.

The Monetization Slide - Backup Slides

The Monetization Slide backup slides should include:

- A slide per revenue stream which shows costs, customers, and income, by quarter, for the last four quarters and the next 12 quarters

- A slide per income stream planned features by revenue stream, plus added costs, for the next 12 quarters

Remember, the goal of the Monetization slide is to explain all the different methods the startup uses to generate revenue.

The Monetization Slide - Construction Checklist

Remember these crucial points about the Monetization Slide startup Story.

- [ ] Use a Master Template
- [ ] Title: MONETIZATION or REVENUE MODEL
- [ ] One or Two Pie Charts
- [ ] If SaaS, Show Revenue break down in MRR/ARR + Setup
- [ ] If Hard-good, show Margins by Sales Channel
- [ ] Current & Next 4-8 Quarters Pie Chart (if applicable)
- [ ] All text is Legible from 100 Feet (33 Meters)
- [ ] Bold Colors (no pastels or light colors)
- [ ] Include CLTV & Retention in months

You can download the Complete Investor Pitch Deck Checklist - *100% FREE* - Click the link below while connected to WiFi.

https://www.ideatogrowth.com/contact-free-download-investor-pitch-deck-checklist

The Monetization Slide - Executive Summary

The Monetization Slide Story and Slide include the below info.

- Use of a Master template (Slide)

- ***MONETIZATION*** or ***REVENUE MODEL*** for the slide title (Slide)

- What diverse types of buyers do you have? (Slide & Story)

- What percentage do you sell direct? (Slide & Story)

- What percentage do you sell through distribution? (Slide & Story)

- How many days between when the startup ships and receipt payment? (Slide & Story)

- Is SaaS as a part of the Monetization? (Slide & Story)

- Is there a Bronze, Silver and Gold SaaS plans? (Slide & Story)

- What annual revenue percentage does each revenue stream generate? (Slide & Story)

- Is there a One-Time Setup charge? (Slide & Story)

- Deliver the Monetization Story in 18-30 seconds (Story)

In the next chapter, I will speak about the eighth part of the startup Story — The Financials Slide.

Chapter Quiz

Q1: Slide title should be "Monetization" or "Revenue Model". [ ] Yes [ ] No

Q2: A table is a better graphics choice vs. a pie chart. [ ] Yes [ ] No

Q3: Show all revenue models, including those not implemented yet. [ ] Yes [ ] No

Q4: What is MRR short for?

Q5: What is ARR short for?

Q6: Combine one-time fees with recurring fees into single MRR. [ ] Yes [ ] No

Q7: Show Margins by Sales Channel. [ ] Yes [ ] No

Q8: Selling thru retailers makes more margin than selling direct to customers. [ ] Yes [ ] No

Q9: What are the two key components that need to be in the Monetization backup slides?

Q10: Always merge hardware and SaaS sales into a single pie chart. [ ] Yes [ ] No

Answers:

https://www.ideatogrowth.com/answers-10-slides-to-startup-funding-success/#slide-7-the-monetization-slide

Chapter Notes

_____

_____

_____

_____

_____

_____

_____

_____

_____

_____

_____

_____

_____

_____

_____

_____

_____

Revenue, Expenses, & Customers

Figure 39 - The Financials Slide

The Financials Slide — Why Is It Important?

Why do startup investors want to hear about the Financials now?

With the Cover Slide, the entrepreneur introduced the startup, themselves and answered the first unspoken startup investor question *Who are you and why am I spending time with you?* (Slide 1).

The startup investors second thought was *What is the Big, Hairy Problem this Startup has Targeted?* (Slide 2)

Next, the startup investors third thought was *Big Problem, but how big is the Market for this Problem?* (Slide 3)

The startup investors fourth thought was *What is the startup Solution for the Market?* (Slide 4)

Next, the startup investors fifth thought was ***Great Solution. How much Market Traction does the startup have?*** (Slide 5)

The startup investors sixth thought was ***What level of Competition does the Startup face and how does the startup Solution stack up against the Competition?*** (Slide 6)

Next, the startup investors seventh thought was ***What are all the Diverse Ways you Generate Revenue?*** (Slide 7)

Now the mind of the startup investor asks, ***What is the Financial Progress and Future Financial Targets?*** (Slide 8)

Numbers for most people tend to be a dull subject. The task of the entrepreneur is to know the essential financials the startup investor wants to hear about on the First-Date. The entrepreneur will review detailed financial plans on a Second-Date, so stay in the shallows for now.

Most entrepreneurs have no degree in finance. Also absent from most entrepreneurs are a bookkeeper and Certified Public Accountant (CPA) skills. For the construction of the Financials Slide, the entrepreneur should seek aid from a financial expert. Ideally, this is a person who the entrepreneur has chosen to serve on the Advisory Board. An alternative is to hire the services of the startup bookkeeper.

The Financials Slide should convey to the startup investor the entrepreneurs understanding of the financial basis of the operation of the business. The slide for the Financials should include a few essential numbers from the Balance Sheet, Profit & Loss Statement, and Cash Flow Statement.

While the entrepreneur needs no financial degree, the entrepreneurial CEO should have basic financial literacy. You should get familiar with what a Balance Sheet, Profit & Loss Statement, and Cash flow Statement holds. Take a course or two on Udemy.com, Linda.com., or a similar and learn the fundamentals of finance. Knowledge of the financial basics is necessary for the CEO to be a successful leader.

Startup investors want to know a few economic numbers on a First-Date.

- One: Revenue growth (by quarter)
- Two: Expense growth (by quarter)
- Three: Customer base growth (by quarter)
- Four: Month and year of financial Break-Even

Address these four topics and leave specific points for the post-presentation Q&A and the Second-Date.

Time to learn about the Financials startup Story content.

The Financials Slide - The Startup Story Content

First, write down the critical oral points the startup investor should want to hear when the entrepreneur describes the Financials.

What investor questions should the verbal Story answer?

- Revenue (Last four quarters and forecast the next 12 quarters)

- Expenses (Last four quarters and forecast the next 12 quarters)

- #Customers (Last four quarters and forecast the next 12 quarters)

- Month/Year startup reaches Cash flow Breakeven

Now let us discuss how to Craft and Deliver the Financials startup Story.

The Financials Slide — Craft the Startup Story

Allow me to provide one example of the Financials Slide oral startup pitch which would work well.

Over the last four quarters, GNRB has grown revenue by an average of 86% each quarter.

Over the same period, GNRB number of Customers has grown at a quarterly compounded rate of 65%, which reflects more Customers have chosen higher-priced products.

Over the next two years, GNRB forecasts a compounded quarterly customer growth of 88% as the sales growth and sales channels expand.

GNRB expects the compounded quarterly Revenue growth to increase to 117% as new Clients to choose the higher priced products.

GNRB estimates the average customer lifetime value to be two years and USD 3800.

GNRB expect to have the first month of profitability in November of this year.

Now it is time to discuss how to create the Financials Slide.

The Financials Slide — Create the Slide

Most Financial slides I see from entrepreneurs are a mess. Typically, I see a Financials Slide which resembles this next image:

Figure 40 - Bad Financials Slide Example

Entrepreneurs, please avoid the construction of a Financials Slide like this. Bury a slide like this one deep into the Backup Slides. The development of a Financials Slide like the one above will cause the entrepreneur to lose the startup investors' attention instantly.

Additionally, this slide design violates my Best Practices rule to use as little text and numbers as possible.

The Financials slide should use a side-by-side bar and line chart.

- What investor questions should the slide answer?
- Revenue (by quarter for the last four quarters and next 12 quarters - green bars on chart)

- Expenses (by quarter for the previous four quarters and next 12 quarters - red bars on chart)

- Total number of customers (for the previous four quarters and the next 12 quarters - Line graph)

- A big arrow with the month and year of break-even

The image at the start of this chapter is an excellent example of one of the companies I coach. Here is an excellent example slide again.

This excellent example slide includes all the four crucial metrics I mentioned.

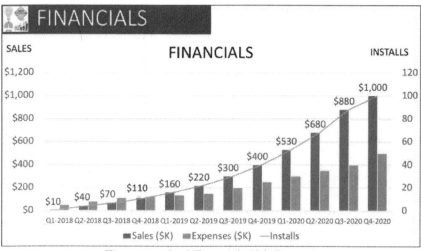

Figure 41 - Good Financials Slide Example

This bar and line chart slide format is much friendlier and more focused than the earlier giant table of numbers bad Financials slide example. With the exclusion of an accounting nerd, your startup investor will be more impressed with this slide.

Now it is time to discuss the Financials Backup Slides.

The Financials Slide - Backup Slides

The Financials Slide backup slides should include:

- Monthly Revenues - Direct, Distribution, Other - Last 12 months and next three years

- Quarterly Revenues - Direct, Distribution, Other - Last four quarters and next 12 quarters

- Monthly Expenses - Last 12 months and following three years

- Quarterly Expenses - Last four quarters and next 12 quarters

- Monthly Product Margins - Last 12 months and the next three years

- Quarterly Margins (by-product) - Last four quarters and next 12 quarters

- By Customer Sales Slide - Last 12 months and following three years

- Sales Slide for each big Customer- Last four quarters and next 12 quarters

- Customer Acquisition Costs (CAC) - Direct, Distribution, Other - Last four quarters and next 12 quarters

- Customer Lifetime Value (CLTV) - Last four quarters and next 12 quarters

Remember, the goal of the Financials slide is to highlight the current and planned Customer Sales, Expenses and Customer growth rate.

The Financials Slide - Construction Checklist

Remember these crucial points about the Financials Slide startup Story.

- ☐ Use a Master Template
- ☐ Title: FINANCIALS
- ☐ Revenue (by quarter for the last four quarters and next 12 quarters - Green-bar Graph)
- ☐ Expenses (by quarter for the previous four quarters and next 12 quarters - Red-bar Graph)
- ☐ Total Customers (by quarter for the previous four quarters and next 12 quarters - Line Graph)
- ☐ Arrow to month and year of break-even
- ☐ All text is LEGIBLE from 100 Feet (33 Meters)
- ☐ Bold Colors (no pastels or light colors)
- ☐ Have backup slides with added Financial details (Story)

You can download the Complete Investor Pitch Deck Checklist - **100% FREE** - Click the link below while connected to WiFi.

https://www.ideatogrowth.com/contact-free-download-investor-pitch-deck-checklist

The Financials Slide - Executive Summary

The Financials Slide Story and Slide include the below info.

- Use of a Master template (Slide)

- **_FINANCIALS_** for the slide title (Slide)

- One: Revenue growth (by quarter) (Slide & Story)

- Two: Expense growth (by quarter) (Slide & Story)

- Three: Customer base growth (by quarter) (Slide & Story)

- Four: Month and year of financial Break-Even (Slide & Story)

- Deliver the Financials Story in 18-30 seconds (Story)

- Minimize Text - Use Images to Tell the startup Story (Slide)

- The text is Legible from 100 Feet (33 Meters) (Slide)

- Bold Colors (no pastels or light colors) (Slide)

ANGEL INVESTORS TO VENTURE CAPITAL
10 SLIDES TO STARTUP FUNDING SUCCESS

In the next chapter, I will speak about the ninth part of the startup Story — The Team Slide.

Also, be sure to check out the Resources page for helpful downloads! There is also a link to save you dozens of hours building your own Investor Pitch Deck Slide template. For book buyers I include a discount code that will save you $$$.

Click <u>RESOURCES</u> to jump to the download page now.

Chapter Quiz

Q1: What should the slide title be?

Q2: Show revenue by month. [ ] Yes [ ] No

Q3: Show revenue & expenses by quarter for the previous 4 quarters. [ ] Yes [ ] No

Q4: Show revenue and expense forecast for 5 years. [ ] Yes [ ] No

Q5: Don't include an indicator of break-even. [ ] Yes [ ] No

Q6: What is CAC short for?

Q7: Use Q1 - Q12 to show quarters. Don't show years. [ ] Yes [ ] No

Q8: Use a table to show revenue & expenses. [ ] Yes [ ] No

Q9: Only revenue and expenses matter. [ ] Yes [ ] No

Q10: What are the 4 key messages to deliver on this slide?

Q11: You need detailed financials in the backups to support this slide. [ ] Yes [ ] No

Answers:

https://www.ideatogrowth.com/answers-10-slides-to-startup-funding-success/#slide-8-the-financials-slide

Chapter Notes

Those Who Will Create a Successful Startup

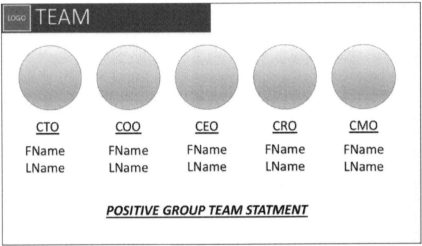

Figure 42 - The Team Slide

The Team Slide — Why Is It Important?

Why do startup investors want to hear about the Team now?

With the Cover Slide, the entrepreneur introduced the startup, themselves and answered the first unspoken startup investor question *Who are you and why am I spending time with you?* (Slide 1).

The startup investors second thought was *What is the Big, Hairy Problem this Startup has Targeted?* (Slide 2)

Next, the startup investors third thought was *Big Problem, but how big is the Market for this Problem?* (Slide 3)

The startup investors fourth thought was *What is the startup Solution for the Market?* (Slide 4)

Next, the startup investors fifth thought was ***Great Solution. How much Market Traction does the startup have?*** (Slide 5)

The startup investors sixth thought was ***What level of Competition does the Startup face and how does the startup Solution stack up against the Competition?*** (Slide 6)

Next, the startup investors seventh thought was ***What are all the Diverse Ways you Generate Revenue?*** (Slide 7)

The startup investors eighth thought was ***What is the Financial Progress and Future Financial Targets?*** (Slide 8)

Now the mind of the startup investor asks, ***Who is on the Team that will Build a Successful Company?*** (Slide 9)

The CEO must review each management members LinkedIn profile. If a management team member does not have a LinkedIn profile, they need to build a good one. Be sure the image is current and proper (no casual shots). Be sure the content follows best practices as outlined by many prominent business coaches and other professionals.

The CEO should also examine other social media sites of the management team members. Be sure Facebook users are unable to see derogatory and unprofessional content. Have the management team member remove any images of themselves in which they consume alcoholic beverages or images which provide an under-the-influence appearance. Have the team member transfer any videos which show them engaged in actions most Moms would find objectional.

Have the team member remove similar content for all other social media sites such as Instagram, Snapchat and other places which get media attention.

The entrepreneur needs to recognize the writings of strong personal positions of a political or religious nature can hurt an otherwise excellent team from successful fundraising. While the use of this censorship may be personally offensive, lack of such constraint could cost the Company investors.

Time to learn about the Team startup Story content.

The Team Slide - The Startup Story Content

First, write down the critical oral points the startup investor should want to hear when the entrepreneur describes the Team.

Start first with who should be on the Team Slide.

Remember I mentioned in the chapter, The 4 Stages of a Successful Business, the three crucial positions in every startup.

- CEO - Who will Lead the team?
- CTO - Who will Design & Build the Product?
- CRO - Who will Sell the Products and Services?

The CEO (Chief Executive Officer) is the team member responsible for the leadership of the Company. This person may hold the alternative or added title of President. All Executive management members report to the CEO. The CEO reports to the Board of Directors (Board or BoD).

The CTO (Chief Technical Officer) is the team member responsible for the MVP design. This person may hold the alternative title of VP of Engineering or VP of Product Development. Often in the first stages of the startup, this person may also have the responsibilities of the COO (Chief Operations Office) or VP of Operations. The COO position usually oversees the manufacture of the startup Products.

The CRO (Chief Revenue Officer) is the management team member responsible for the sale of the Products and Services of the Company. This person may hold the alternative title of VP of Sales.

The slide has three crucial items to speak to about each member of the management team.

1. Full Name

2. Business Title

3. A word or two about prior relevant roles

The word or two about each management team member should focus on a specific contribution to an earlier, well-known company. If the team member is a recent college graduate, speak to the work and school activities which show they are the right person for the position.

If you have other VP level or higher team members, show images, names, and titles on the slide. Focus on the three mentioned positions and skip the mention of the other team members on the slide.

As the CEO, speak about yourself and abilities last. When the CEO talks about themselves last, this shows the CEO places the management team first in importance. This technique reflects well on the CEO's ability to share the spotlight and lead the team.

If the CEO has not yet hired the CRO (VP of Sales) or CTO (VP of Product Development) team members, you still need to speak to these critical positions. Ideally, as CEO you have found a person to do the job on a part-time basis who will come on board full-time upon the completion of funds.

Tell the startup investors if you have an Advisory Board and if one of the members is acting in one of the three critical management roles. Show the Advisory Board members image, name, and include the word Interim in front of CTO or CRO position. Include the title Advisory Board Member as a second title.

If a top management position is unfilled, say so. Stating the need to fill an executive management role is an opportunity for the right startup investor who is interested in the Company to step up and help with an introduction.

Again, I urge the entrepreneur to fill all three of the crucial management positions before you begin startup investor pitches. Many startup investors, myself included, avoid meetings with solopreneurs. Even startup investors who will meet with solopreneurs, most fail to provide Seed Funding until these three crucial management positions have at least part-timers in the roles.

Remember, most startup investors invest in people first, and ideas second.

If you have an Advisory Board or a formal Board of Directors, I urge you to create a backup slide in a similar format for each.

Now let us discuss how to Craft and Deliver the Team startup Story.

The Team Slide — Craft the Startup Story

Allow me to provide one example of the Team Slide oral startup pitch which would work well.

Now I would like to introduce my incredible team!

Mary Simmons is the Chief Technical Officer (CTO). She has built websites and mobile applications for more than ten years. She was at Square Space where she was VP of Technology in charge of Template Development.

John Myers is the VP of Sales. He has more than 20 years of Sales experience at companies which includes IBM, Incorp, and Cisco.

I am Jim Johnson and serve as the CEO. My experience includes VP of Business Development at Sun Microsystems and Director of Business Development at IBM.

Short, sweet, and focused. The entrepreneur has shown the startup investor you can assemble a crucial rock-star management startup team. The entrepreneur has also minimized startup investor concern if you dropped dead, their investment would disappear. The startup investors funds are in the hands of a competent team.

Now it is time to discuss how to create the Team Slide.

The Team Slide — Create the Slide

Most Team Slides I see from entrepreneurs are dull and incomplete.

Often, Team Slides I see is a list of names. Sometimes the Team Slide is a group image.

Sometimes no Team Slide exists because there is no team. Sometimes, the startup has a single team member - the startup entrepreneur!

The Team Slide should show who the management team is. Use a simple color headshot. Usually, the image of each team member from their LinkedIn profile is an excellent usable image.

Below the image put the full name and below that, the management title.

Below the management team images, names and titles, the slide should have some text which speaks to the collective skills of the management team. Later the entrepreneur will refer to these words, but they will avoid reading the words aloud. The few words will support the one to two sentence statements you made about each team member.

- Who is the CEO (Image, Name, Title)?

- Who is the CTO (Image, Name, Title)?

- Who is the CRO (Image, Name, Title)?

- Who are any other VP team members (Image, Name, Title)?

Time to examine how to avoid construction of the Team Slide.

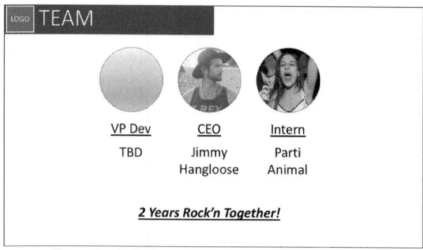

Figure 43 - An Inadequate Example of a Management Team Slide

What above is unhelpful at impressing an Investor? Here is what I see.

- Crucial management team member VP of Product Development is unidentified.

- CEO image appears unprofessional

- VP of Sales image appears unprofessional

- The Positive overall statement about the management team is inadequate

Time to examine a more positive Team Slide example:

Figure 44 - Good Example of a Team Slide

The above management team slide example has gone beyond the management team members of CEO, CRO, and CTO. This slide creates a formidable management team statement.

If you were a startup investor, which slides team is the wiser startup investment?

If any of the three crucial positions are unfilled, the entrepreneur will still show the startup management position on the slide. Insert an empty caricature for the image and a TBD for the name. Show the position title. Speak to the fact you recognize this is a crucial management position the CEO must hire. If the CEO needs help filling this position, the First-Date is an inappropriate tie to share this fact, unless the startup investor interrupts and asks you directly. If the startup investor does ask, I recommend saying you are open to speaking with all qualified candidates the startup investor can endorse.

Now it is time to discuss the Team Backup Slides.

The Team Slide - Backup Slides

The Team Slide backup slides should include:

- One slide per startup Management member which includes:
- Full Name
- Startup Title
- LinkedIn URL
- Email
- Current Salary and post-investment salary
- One slide of the entire Advisory Board which includes:
- Full Name
- One slide per Advisory Board member which includes:
- Full Name
- LinkedIn URL
- Email
- One slide with the whole Board of Directors which includes:
- Full Name
- LinkedIn URL
- One slide per Board of Directors member which includes:
- Full Name
- LinkedIn URL
- Email

Remember, the goal of the Team slide is to highlight the strengths of the core team and put a face to each management team member.

The Team Slide - Construction Checklist

Remember these crucial points about the Team Slide startup Story.

- [ ] Use a Master Template
- [ ] Title: TEAM
- [ ] CEO Professional Headshot, Name, Title
- [ ] VP Sales Professional Headshot, Name, Title
- [ ] VP Development Professional Headshot, Name, Title
- [ ] Have a statement about the overall team experience level
- [ ] Speak about the team first and yourself last
- [ ] All text is Legible from 100 Feet (33 Meters)
- [ ] Leave off the slide: Email Address
- [ ] Leave off the slide: LinkedIn URL
- [ ] Leave off the slide: startup Website URL
- [ ] Leave off the slide: All Phone Numbers
- [ ] Leave off the slide: Twitter Address
- [ ] Leave off the slide: Facebook URL

You can download the Complete Investor Pitch Deck Checklist - **100% FREE** - Click the link below while connected to WiFi.

https://www.ideatogrowth.com/contact-free-download-investor-pitch-deck-checklist

The Team Slide - Executive Summary

The Team Slide Story and Slide include the below info.

- Use of a Master template (Slide)

- **TEAM** for the slide title (Slide)

- Who is the CEO (Image, Name, Title)? (Slide & Story)

- Who is the CTO (Image, Name, Title)? (Slide & Story)

- Who is the CRO (Image, Name, Title)? (Slide & Story)

- Who are any other VP team members (Image, Name, Title)? (Slide)

- Deliver the Team Story in 18-30 seconds (Story)

- Minimize Text - Use Images to Tell the startup Story (Slide)

- The text is Legible from 100 Feet (33 Meters) (Slide)

- Bold Colors (no pastels or light colors) (Slide)

In the next chapter, I will speak about the tenth part of the startup Story — The Ask Slide.

SLIDE 9 — THE TEAM SLIDE

Chapter Quiz

Q1: The CEO image should appear front and center. [ ] Yes [ ] No

Q2: Include the BoD members on the slide. [ ] Yes [ ] No

Q3: Use funny headshots of the management. [ ] Yes [ ] No

Q4: Include phone, email, and LinkedIn URL's. [ ] Yes [ ] No

Q5: Include a background bio with each headshot. [ ] Yes [ ] No

Q6: Make a backup slide for every staff and BoD member with all contact and social profile URL's. [ ] Yes [ ] No

Q7: Use a font easily read from 100 feet. [ ] Yes [ ] No

Q8: Use a single tagline to describe the joint skills of the management team. [ ] Yes [ ] No

Q9: Use the slide title "My Staff". [ ] Yes [ ] No

Q10: The speaker (CEO) should verbalize their name first or last? [ ] First [ ] Last

Answers:

https://www.ideatogrowth.com/answers-10-slides-to-startup-funding-success/#slide-9-the-team-slide

Chapter Notes

Investment Needs for Startup Success

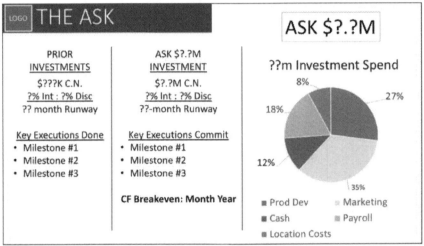

Figure 45 - The Ask Slide

The Ask Slide — Why Is It Important?

Why do startup investors want to hear about the Ask last?

With the Cover Slide, the entrepreneur introduced the startup, themselves and answered the first unspoken startup investor question *Who are you and why am I spending time with you?* (Slide 1).

The startup investors second thought was *What is the Big, Hairy Problem this Startup has Targeted?* (Slide 2)

Next, the startup investors third thought was *Big Problem, but how big is the Market for this Problem?* (Slide 3)

The startup investors fourth thought was *What is the startup Solution for the Market?* (Slide 4)

Next, the startup investors fifth thought was ***Great Solution. How much Market Traction does the startup have*** (Slide 5)

The startup investors sixth thought was ***What level of Competition does the Startup face and how does the startup Solution stack up against the Competition?*** (Slide 6)

Next, the startup investors seventh thought was ***What are all the Diverse Ways you Generate Revenue?*** (Slide 7)

The startup investors eighth thought was ***What is the Financial Progress and Future Financial Targets?*** (Slide 8)

Next, the startup investors ninth thought was ***Who is on the Team that will Build a Successful Company?*** (Slide 9)

Now the mind of the startup investor asks, ***How much Funding does the startup Need for this Round?*** (Slide 10)

Most Ask Slides I see from entrepreneurs are slim on details. Often the slide states, ***I need USD 1M.*** The rational response from startup investors is ***What do I get?***

Other Ask Slides I have seen claim ***I need USD 1M, and I am valuing the startup at a post-investment valuation of USD 5M.*** The response from startup investor is ***OK; you have no sales, no customers, no Minimum Viable Product (MVP). No accomplishments and you are offering me 20% of the startup?*** An Ask Slide having such limited information shows the entrepreneur is inexperienced.

Entrepreneurs should learn from these examples and avoid these types of mistakes.

Yes, some early-stage companies do get ridiculously high valuations at the Seed or Series A Stage. One can read about these ridiculously high valuations in the press.

Hey, this should be me too! This idea is a natural thought.

The reality is there are many reasons why another startup in the same or similar space, was able to fundraise at a high valuation. However, most of these reasons are undeterminable by those outside of the transaction.

A few reasons for high Seed or Series A valuations are:

- Successful earlier exit by one or more of the founders
- High current sales or big contracts for sales
- Expressed future acquisition interest from a big company
- Strong interest by managing partners at the venture firm
- Friends and Family startup investors
- Inexperienced startup investors

The critical point for the entrepreneur to remember is you need to find a startup investor willing to fund the startup and who has the contacts to help you get the next investment round. If the entrepreneur over-prices the startup in an investment round, the next investment round may become impossible.

If the entrepreneur over-prices the round, there is a high probability of a ***down-round***. In laypeople terms, a down-round is one where the equivalent stock value of the investment made by the last investment round is worth less in value than the new investment round.

A ***down-round*** is a tough situation for the startup and the management team. Proper early planning of how much investment the startup needs at each investment round helps avoid this fatal miss-step.

Time to learn about the Ask startup Story content.

The Ask Slide - The Startup Story Content

These are the crucial points to cover on the Ask presentation.

- Earlier Funds-Raised

- Top Three Previous Investments Accomplishments

- Investment Sought for Current Round

- Committed startup investor Amount for Current Round

- If the Current Investment Round is a Convertible Note:

- Principal Amount

- Interest Rate (~ 5% to 8%)

- Maturity (~ 12 to 24 months)

- Discount (~ 20% to 25%)

- If the Current Investment Round is a Stock Purchase:

- Number of new Shares to be Issued

- The Price per Share

- The Total Shares Outstanding (post-investment)

- Pre and Post Investment Round startup Valuation

- Use of Funds (up to top eight areas (in % dollars))

- Months of Investment Runway

- Runway Top Three Accomplishments to Complete

I will discuss each of these items next in detail.

Previous Funds-Raised

Previous Funds-Raised refers to the total dollars previously invested in the startup. Previous Funds-Raised refers to any cash investment in the startup made by anyone. Previous Funds-Raised does not include *sweat equity*.

For readers not familiar with the term *Sweat Equity* it refers to the time, equipment, and other resources founders and others have invested in the startup. The Previous Funds-Raised calculation does not include these efforts, equipment, and other non-cash items.

Top Three Previous Investments Accomplishments

As a startup investor, I have never seen this crucial information shown on any slide or shared without prompting by a startup investor. If someone has put cash into the Company, the entrepreneur should be able to point to three significant accomplishments they achieved with those invested dollars. If the entrepreneur is not able to, why should any new startup investor expect the entrepreneur to meet three essential achievements with a new investment?

Investment Sought for Current Round

This item is simple. How many dollars does the startup need to fundraise from startup investors in this new round?

Committed Investor Amount for Current Round

Another simple item. How many dollars have startup investors committed to this new round?

If a startup investor has not signed the Term Sheet, there are not any committed dollars from startup investors. The entrepreneur can say they have a certain number of dollars of investment inquired about by interested startup investors.

If Current Investment Round is a Convertible Note:

If the new investment round uses a Convertible Note or SAFE Note, there are four numbers startup investors want to know at the First-Date startup pitch.

- Principal Amount

The Principal Amount of a convertible note is the total invested dollar amount by the noteholders. Unlike most other debt instruments, a Convertible Note issued with an original issue discount (a price that is less than the face value of the instrument) is uncommon.

Read more on this topic in the Getting to the Funding Close chapter.

- Interest Rate (~ 5% to 8%)

The Interest Rate on a Convertible Note accrues on the investment while the note stays outstanding (i.e., until a conversion event or demand upon maturity). Interest can either be a simple rate per annum or compounded quarterly or annually.

Read more on this topic in the Getting to the Funding Close chapter.

- Maturity (~ 12 to 24 Months)

The Maturity of the Note relates to the time when repayment of the note, plus interest, is due to the noteholder. Typically, a note matures 12 or 24 months after investment in the Company.

Read more on this topic in the Getting to the Funding Close chapter.

- Discount (~ 20% to 25%)

A Discount (Rate) is a method of compensation enhancement used by startups to compensate Seed Round startup investors for the acceptance of a higher risk than startup investors who fund at a later round.

Convertible Notes offer noteholders the benefit of converting into preferred equity at a discount to the price paid by the later startup investors at a qualified financial event.

The standard discount offered to convertible noteholders in a Seed Round is in the range of 20% to 25%.

Read more on this topic in the Getting to the Funding Close chapter.

If Current Investment Round is a Stock Purchase

If the new investment round is via startup stock, there are four numbers startup investors want to know at the First-Date startup pitch.

- Number of New Shares to be Issued

Express the number of newly issued shares to as a number.

- The Price per Share

Express the Price per Share as a currency number. Price per share is the price per share of the new stock to be issued in this investment round.

- The Total Shares Outstanding (post-investment)

Express the Total Shares Outstanding (post-investment) as a number. Total Shares Outstanding (post-investment) is the total number of shares outstanding after the close of this investment round.

- Pre and Post-Round Startup Company Valuation

Express the pre and post-round startup Valuation as a currency number. Pre and post-Round startup Valuation is the total valuation of the startup before and after the close of this investment round.

Use-of-Funds

The entrepreneur can best express the Use-of-Funds with a pie chart on the Ask Slide. The Use of Funds Pie Chart should have readable labels. I recommend the entrepreneur show five to ten buckets of spending.

- Facilities (Rent, Desks, Chairs)
- Equipment & Software (Computers, Printers, CMS)
- Product Inventory
- Website Development (Not SaaS part)
- Advertising (Paid)
- Product Development (Hardware and SaaS)
- Product Testing (outside services)
- Product Launch Marketing
- Patents & Trademarks
- Salaries (staff vs. management breakout)

Months of Investment Runway

Months of Investment Runway is the period while in which you will spend the investment dollars.

Runways Top Three Accomplishments to Complete

The Runways Top Three Accomplishments to complete while in the new runway timeframe is one of the most critical pieces of information on this slide. Startup investors are busy people. If the entrepreneur can get the startup investor to remember three essential items about the investment, the entrepreneur is doing an excellent job.

Often this is the time when the startup investor makes the critical decision to continue, or not to continue, with an investment opportunity. Here the entrepreneur must answer the question:

Will my investment enables the accomplishment of important tasks which will allow the startup to get the next investment round at a higher valuation?

The entrepreneur needs to write down three crucial milestones the startup will complete before the start of the next investment round. These essential milestones often center on one of these topics.

- Customer growth
- Revenue growth
- Expense reduction
- Current Market penetration growth and New Markets
- Margin improvement
- Financial Breakeven achievement

Now let us discuss how to Craft and Deliver the Ask startup Story.

The Ask Slide — Craft the Startup Story

Allow me to provide one example of the Ask Slide oral startup pitch which would work well.

QRTS has fundraised USD 50K in the form of a Convertible Note from Friends and Family. The Interest Rate is 5% with a 20% discount. This investment round QRTS will fundraise a USD 150K as a Convertible Note under the same terms.

The three founders hold all the startup stock in equal percentages with 10% set aside for new hires. This USD 150K investment round provides nine months of runway.

The team commits to the completion of three crucial tasks. First, reach USD 25K MRR. Second, roll out our services into Atlanta GA and Miami FL with USD 10K+ MRR each. Three, release the iOS and Android versions of the service.

I have seen a lot of great entrepreneurs fumble the ball on the 1-yard line, which is my football analogy for what the Ask Slide represents in the First-Date startup pitch. This slide of the Investor Pitch Deck takes a lot of work on the part of the entrepreneur. Do the job, and you increase the likelihood of a successful outcome.

Now it is time to discuss how to create the Ask Slide.

The Ask Slide - Create the Slide

Before I show you the right way to construct the Ask Slide, allow me to show you how not to build one.

In the slide below the entrepreneur has limited the information they are providing to the startup investor.

- Investment Sought for Current Round
- The type of security (Convertible Note)
- The Runway
- A Single Task Commitment

This Ask Slide is woefully inadequate for any startup investor to whom I have ever spoken.

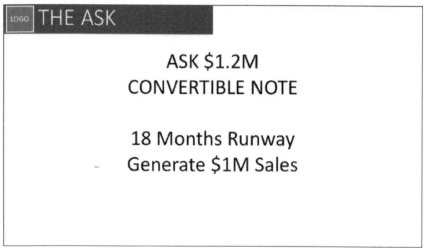

Figure 46 - The Ask Slide - Bad Example

Time to take the content we discussed and turn it into an informative Ask slide like the example I show next.

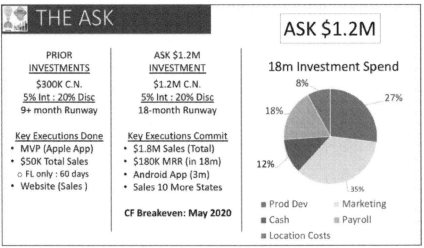

Figure 47 - The Ask Slide - A Great Example

Have we covered all the crucial information?

✓ Total Previous Funds Raised

✓ Top Three Previous Investments Accomplishments

✓ Investment Sought for Current Round

✓ Committed Investor Amount for Current Round

✓ If Current Investment Round is a Convertible Note:

• Principal Amount

• Interest Rate (~ 5% to 8%)

• Maturity (~ 12 to 24 months)

• Discount (~ 20% to 25%)

✓ Use of Funds (up to top eight areas (in % dollars))

✓ Months of Investment Runway

✓ Runways Top Three Accomplishments to Complete

Now it is time to discuss the Ask Backup Slides.

The Ask Slide - Backup Slides

The Ask Slide backup slides should include:

- Funds invested, by startup investor, with the date of funds transfer

- Each startup investors Name, Email, LinkedIn URL, Phone

- A breakdown of earlier Use of Funds investments

- An analysis of the Use of Funds for the current round

Remember, the goal of the Ask slide is to highlight the investments already made and needed in the Company, along with the three crucial prior tasks and three critical new tasks, plus the use of funds.

The Ask Slide - Construction Checklist

- ☐ Use a Master Template
- ☐ Title: ASK
- ☐ Total Previous Fund-Raises
- ☐ Top Three Previous Investments Accomplishments
- ☐ Investment Sought for Current Round
- ☐ Committed startup investor Amount for Current Round
- ☐ If Current Investment Round is a Convertible Note:
- ☐ Principal Amount
- ☐ Interest Rate (~ 5% to 8%)
- ☐ Maturity (~ 12 to 24 months)
- ☐ Discount (~ 20% to 25%)
- ☐ If Current Investment Round is a Stock Purchase:
- ☐ Number of new Shares to be Issued
- ☐ The Price per Share
- ☐ The Total Shares Outstanding (post-investment)
- ☐ Pre and Post Investment Round startup Valuation
- ☐ Use of Funds (up to top eight areas (in % dollars))
- ☐ Months of Investment Runway
- ☐ Runways Top Three Accomplishments to Complete

You can download the Complete Investor Pitch Deck Checklist - *100% FREE* - Click the link below while connected to WiFi.

https://www.ideatogrowth.com/contact-free-download-investor-pitch-deck-checklist

The Ask Slide - Executive Summary

The Ask Slide Story and Slide include the below info.

- Use of a Master template (Slide)

- *ASK* for the slide title (Slide)

- Total Previous Funds-Raises (Slide & Story)

- Top Three Previous Investments Goals (Slide & Story)

- Investment Sought for Current Round (Slide & Story)

- Committed Amount for Current Round (Slide & Story)

- If Current Investment Round is a Convertible Note:

- Principal Amount (Slide & Story)

- Interest Rate (~ 5% to 8%) (Slide)

- Maturity (~ 12 to 24 months) (Slide)

- Discount (~ 20% to 25%) (Slide)

- If Current Investment Round is a Stock Purchase,

- Price per Share & Number of new Shares to be Issued (Slide)

- The Total Shares Outstanding (post-investment) (Slide)

- Pre and Post Investment Round Valuation (Slide)

- Use of Funds (up to top eight areas (in % dollars)) (Slide)

- Months of Investment Runway (Slide & Story)

- Runway Top Three Goals (Slide & Story)

- Deliver the Ask Story in 18-30 seconds (Story)

In the next chapter, I will speak about the next part of the startup Story — Telling the Startup Story on The Clock.

Chapter Quiz

Q1: Slide title is "Investment Required". [ ] Yes [ ] No

Q2: Be vague on whether you are selling stock or requesting a loan to maximize investor interest. [ ] Yes [ ] No

Q3: Leave off earlier monies raised and related accomplishments. [ ] Yes [ ] No

Q4: Share the top 5 to 8 categories of use of the investment / loan in a pie chart. [ ] Yes [ ] No

Q5: Keep secret all investor commitments for the current round. [ ] Yes [ ] No

Q6: If selling stock, always show the offering as post investment ownership percentage. [ ] Yes [ ] No

Q7: Always show the number of months of runway the investment will provide prior to needing to raise added capital. [ ] Yes [ ] No

Q8: Always show the top 10 accomplishments the investment will allow the company team to carry out. [ ] Yes [ ] No

Q9: Why is this slide the "last" presented slide?

Q10: Show the forecasted breakeven month and year (even if outside the runway window). [ ] Yes [ ] No

Answers:

https://www.ideatogrowth.com/answers-10-slides-to-startup-funding-success/#slide-10-the-ask-slide

Chapter Notes

_____

_____

_____

_____

_____

_____

_____

_____

_____

_____

_____

_____

_____

_____

_____

_____

_____

Tell the Startup Story on the Clock

Figure 48 - The 3 to 10 Minute Pitch

Congratulations. If you have read the earlier chapters once, before getting into Crafting the startup Story for each of the ten main slides, it is time to discuss how to tell the startup Story on the clock.

Typically, the entrepreneur will have 90 seconds to six minutes to share the startup Story at an Investor Pitch Event. In 2018 many pitch events shifted to a 2-1/2 minute (150 seconds) format. This same 10 Slides to Startup Funding Success format will fit into a 90 second presentation. The art is in the parts of your story that you share!

If you have followed my earlier advice, you should have crafted the startup Story for each slide to encompass about three to ten focused sentences. For a shorter startup pitch period, the entrepreneur will cut sentences from each slide. Since you have planned for this, the startup Story should sound as strong, but with some of the details left out.

Done correctly, this can work to the advantage. Leaving out the right details, while giving others, can be an enticing tease to a startup investor. The result is the startup investor will look to speak with the entrepreneur after the presentation. This technique can help the entrepreneur identify quality startup investors from a tire-kicker startup investor who wastes valuable time at startup-investor pitch events.

Most startup-investor pitch events have no questions while the entrepreneur present. Startup investor questions usually occur after all the entrepreneurs have presented. Often there is a separate room with tables the entrepreneurs and startup investors can meet and have a brief Q&A session.

What if the entrepreneur has a 30-minute one-on-one First-Date meeting with an Investor? Surprise. The entrepreneur still should use a maximum of ten minutes to share the startup Story (do the startup pitch).

What? If I have a thirty-minute appointment, why should I startup pitch for three to ten minutes?

We were born with two ears and one mouth, and each is used best in this proportion is an old and wise saying.

Per this saying, in a thirty-minute appointment, you should be startup pitching for ten minutes and listening for twenty minutes.

The entrepreneur asks, *Why should I listen so much? I feel like I should do more startup pitching?*

THE 3 TO 10 MINUTE INVESTOR PITCH

Remember this is a First-Date. A big part of the First-Date is you and the startup investor each deciding as to whether there should be a Second-Date. On the First-Date you need time to answer crucial questions from the startup investor, and the entrepreneur needs time to ask essential questions of the startup investor.

If the entrepreneur has thirty minutes for the startup investor pitch meeting, you should use no more than the first ten minutes to do the startup investor pitch. Reserve the second ten minutes to answer questions from the startup investor. The last ten minutes of the meeting you should use to ask questions you have for the startup investor.

These last ten minutes of the 30-minute schedule, the entrepreneur needs to ask questions to determine if this startup investor is worth more of their time.

What are the 10 crucial questions to ask the startup investor?

- Based on this first meeting, is the startup investor interested in a Second-Date?
- What experience level does the startup investor have in the space?
- How big is the startup investors fund?
- How much dry-powder does the startup investor have to invest in the first investment round with a new startup?
- What is the typical investment amount made in companies at a similar stage by the Investor?

- For the requested funds, does the startup investor prefer to take the full ask or partner with another startup investor?

- Does the startup investor prefer to lead or follow?

- Who are other preferred partner investors?

- What Due Diligence process does the startup investor follow and how many weeks and meetings are involved?

- What is the Due Diligence Process and what are the information needs of the investor?

This list scratches the surface of the information the entrepreneur will want to discover. However, the entrepreneur should try to get answers to these crucial questions while in the First-Date.

Why these questions?

To stop the entrepreneur from getting their hopes too high and wasting time!

The Entrepreneur Rarely Hears the Word *NO*

It is rare for startup investors to say; ***No, I have no interest.***

Why?

Because few startup investors want to close the door to investment, even to an investment which may be an unwise fit. If you get ***NO*** response from a startup investor, this often means the entrepreneur will never reach out to this startup investor for a future startup idea.

Because it is rare for startup investors to say **NO** to an entrepreneur, often a startup investor words or tone might sound like **YES** even if the startup investor has no investment interest.

Entrepreneurs will sometimes feel like a startup investor is on the hook when all the startup investor has done, is like a fish, bumped against the fishing line. When the fish hits the fishing line, many entrepreneurs will slow or even stop fishing for startup investors.

Here is my strongest recommendation. Always be aggressively fishing (for startup investors) until the fish (investment dollars) is in the boat (bank).

Most experienced salespersons will tell you to create a sense of urgency to help get a buyer off the fence and landed as a paying customer.

When deciding to focus energies on a startup investor, the entrepreneur must be sure the startup investors sense of urgency aligns with the entrepreneurs.

A terrific way to ensure alignment of interests is to have competition. An example is the realty business. Great realtors strive to have multiple qualified buyers who want to buy the house. When a realtor achieves this goal, the realtor will often start a bidding war to lift the selling price.

The homeowner can also use this multiple buyer interest technique to get more favorable sales terms for your house. As the seller, you might you want a 10-day all cash close. Tight purchase requirements will drop buyers who require a bank loan from a bank for which the buyer may fail to qualify.

Entrepreneurs seeking multiple startup investors can have several positive outcomes.

- Higher Valuation

- Quicker Close

- Better Terms

- Hooking the Next Investment Round Investor

What do I mean by *Hooking the Next Investment Round Investor?* When there are multiple startup investors interested in investing in the current investment round, there may be startup investors who will be unable to participate in the current series. The startup investors who do not choose to participate in the current investment round may want to invest in the next investment cycle.

Handle the unchosen startup investors from the current investment round with the greatest of respect. The entrepreneur should inform the unchosen startup investors that they should consider investing in the next investment round in 12 to 18 months.

The startup should keep all unchosen startup investors appraised of the progress each month via a company newsletter. The CEO should also send a personal email each quarter to keep the unchosen startup investors as a warm lead for the next investment round.

In the next chapter, I will speak about the pitch follow-up — Investor Q&A.

Chapter Quiz

Q1: What are the 10 crucial questions to ask the startup investor?

Q2: What is the primary goal of the first-date?

Q3: An Entrepreneur should focus all their energies on the first potential investor that says, "I'm interested". [ ] Yes [ ] No

Q4: An investor will always tell you if they're interested or not after the first-date. [ ] Yes [ ] No

Q5: You have a 30-minute first-date scheduled. You should plan on pitching for 20-minutes. [ ] Yes [ ] No

Q6: What are 4 upsides to getting investor competition for your round?

Q7: Once you have closed the round, what should you do for all other investors you reached out to?

Q8: The first-date should be all about your pitch and you should not waste time asking questions to the investor about their investment strategies and targeted portfolio interests. [ ] Yes [ ] No

Q9: You should research the VC firm, its partners, and its investments before or after your first-date? [ ] Before [ ] After

Q10: The Angel investor refuses to share any references or companies they've invested in. Should you schedule a first-date?

Answers:

https://www.ideatogrowth.com/answers-10-slides-to-startup-funding-success/#3-to-10-minute-investor-pitch

Chapter Notes

_____

_____

_____

_____

_____

_____

_____

_____

_____

_____

_____

_____

_____

_____

_____

_____

_____

_____

Answer Investor Questions the Right Way

Figure 49 - Handling Investor Q&A

What should the goal be for the post-pitch Investor Q&A session?

Simple. The goal is to set up a bunch of Second-Dates!

I know this statement surprised most of you reading this. The entrepreneur might have thought of the post-pitch Investor Q&A session as little more than an item on the to-do list. The post-pitch Investor Q&A session is the payoff of giving the startup investor pitch.

Now is the opportunity to collect business cards from interested startup investors and encourage each startup investor to ask you to connect after the event for a Second-Date.

If the entrepreneur has done an excellent presentation in front of a group of startup investors who want to invest in your market space, you should attract a considerable startup investor Q&A crowd.

ANGEL INVESTORS TO VENTURE CAPITAL
10 SLIDES TO STARTUP FUNDING SUCCESS

How does the entrepreneur best prepare for an Investor Q&A session after the startup investor pitch held as part of an Accelerator Program or similar startup-investor pitch event?

If the entrepreneur has followed my advice, in the speaker notes you made a list of startup investor questions for each slide topic. Each of those questions includes a short one-to-two sentence answer.

If the format of the Investor Q&A has you positioned at a table with multiple startup investors simultaneously, I recommend the following process.

- Greet each with a smile,

- Followed by a firm handshake,

- Introduce yourself to each startup investor, and

- Exchange business cards before you take questions.

- Thank the startup investors for attending and inform them you will take one question, from each startup investor, in a rotation, to be fair to all involved.

- Lay the startup investors cards on the table in a line.

- Then, one at a time from left-to-right, says the startup investor name and invite that investor to ask a single question.

- For clarity, repeat each question clearly before responding

Rotating through each startup investor prevents any single startup investor from hogging the limited time. Some of the startup investors will be wanting to ask the same question, so this also stops you repeating answers, which wastes time and is dull to most.

Keep the answers short. **_Yes, this is correct,_** is excellent to use for questions seeking affirmation. Avoid expanding on answers unless asked to do so in a follow-up question. **_No, this is incorrect,_** followed by a short one to two sentence correct answer is another great response.

Remember, whether you have a crowd or a single startup investor, the goal is to be short and concise in the responses so that you can answer as many questions as possible. Going into multi-sentence details on an issue is inappropriate now. Show respect to the other startup investors who are waiting to ask an important question. A startup investor who has several questions will wait for multiple turns when there is a short wait because of the entrepreneur's rapid-fire responses.

If more startup investors join the table when you finish a question and before you take the next question, repeat the introduction process, which includes card exchange. Add the new startup investor card to the table at the end of the list, so the new startup investor knows in the question rotation then continue the question rotation to the next startup investor.

In every meeting, there is always a question or two for which the entrepreneur is unprepared. One correct answer exists when the entrepreneur is not 100% sure of the answer. The entrepreneur should respond, **_This is a great question deserving of some thought. Allow me to research your question and get back to you. Is there another question I can address for you today?_**

ANGEL INVESTORS TO VENTURE CAPITAL
10 SLIDES TO STARTUP FUNDING SUCCESS

Experienced startup investors expect some questions to go without an immediate answer. Some experienced startup investors will ask you what I call the **Bull Sh*t** Detector question. The startup investor asks this type of question to see if the entrepreneur understands how to handle a matter in which they are unlikely to know the correct answer.

If you are the CEO and have an Engineering background, the Bull Sh*t Detector question might be related to Finance or Sales - an area in which the CEO should defer to the CFO or VP of Sales. If the CEO wings-it and provides an inadequate or incorrect response, the CEO has failed the **Bull Sh*t** Detector test. The CEO has shown the startup investor there will be times in which the CEO will fail to tell the truth. In a single stroke, the entrepreneur has lost out on a fund-raising opportunity from that startup investors.

The entrepreneur must avoid falling into this trap. Defer questions in which you are unsure of the correct answer. State that this question is one you need to defer to your co-founder to ensure you provide the right answer.

It is also inappropriate to fire up the computer and start showing backup slides, videos or to demo an app. Taking the time to do any of these activities slows down the question rotation process.

Use questions which require detailed answers as a reason to suggest a follow-up a meeting. Remember the primary goal of the Investor Q&A session is to get the Second-Date.

Some startup investors will ask you to email a copy of the startup investor pitch presentation. I recommend against emailing your Investor Pitch Deck to startup investors.

Instead, suggest you schedule a 30-minute one-on-one so you can answer their questions in more detail, and so both parties can better determine if there is a mutual business fit.

Misinterpretation can occur with any presentation without the presence of the entrepreneur to tell the startup Story. Remember, the Investor Pitch Deck is the visual support for the startup Story. Without the entrepreneur to share the startup Story, at best it serves as a memory trigger to a startup investor.

If a startup investor is insistent you send them a copy of the presentation, smile and state you will reach out after the meeting.

If research shows the startup investor meets the qualifications set to be a qualified startup investor, then reach out. The follow-up should be an email requesting a 30-minute coffee meeting. Suggest a couple of near-term dates and time windows, one in the morning and one around the lunch hour, at the startup investors office. Using this follow-up technique gets the ball rolling on nailing down a date at a time while the startup is still fresh in the startup investors mind.

If research shows the startup investor is an unwise fit, the startup needs no further interaction. Entrepreneurs must learn to treat their time like minutes on the clock. Once a minute is gone, regaining that minute is impossible.

ANGEL INVESTORS TO VENTURE CAPITAL
10 SLIDES TO STARTUP FUNDING SUCCESS

In the next chapter, I will speak about what the entrepreneur should do after the startup pitch — The First-Date Pitch Follow-up.

Also, be sure to check out the Resources page for helpful downloads! There is also a link to save you dozens of hours building your own Investor Pitch Deck Slide template. For book buyers I include a discount code that will save you $$$.

Click RESOURCES to jump to the download page now.

Chapter Quiz

Q1: After the pitch a crowd gathers around you. What should you do?

Q2: Should you send investors your pitch? [ ] Yes [ ] No

Q3: You should verbally answer all post pitch question with detailed responses. [ ] Yes [ ] No

Q4: Don't waste time asking for investor business cards. Instead offer yours and ask them to reach out to you. [ ] Yes [ ] No

Q5: If you don't know the answer to an investor question, you should pretend they asked a different question that you know the answer to and respond to that question. [ ] Yes [ ] No

Q6: Should you respond Yes/No to most questions? [ ] Yes [ ] No

Q7: It is best to clearly repeat any question asked in a group setting so all may hear, and the asker is clear as to your response. [ ] Yes [ ] No

Q8: Allow each person to ask all their questions before moving to the next person. [ ] Yes [ ] No

Q9: You should ask for a business card before allowing a participant to ask a question. [ ] Yes [ ] No

Q10: Use the order of the gathered business cards to allow participants to ask questions. [ ] Yes [ ] No

Answers:

https://www.ideatogrowth.com/answers-10-slides-to-startup-funding-success/#post-pitch-q-a-session

Chapter Notes

Entrepreneurs Post First-Date Pitch To-Do List

Figure 50 - What to Do After the Pitch

The Startup Investor Pitch Event has finished. The entrepreneur and co-founders are exhausted. The entrepreneur and the startup team wants to go home and relax.

Wrong. The conclusion of the startup investor pitch is the time to start the post-presentation event follow-up.

The entrepreneur needs to start the Pitch Day same-day follow-up tasks now. What is the required follow-up tasks?

First, write a summary of the event for you and to share with the team. The startup CEO should have at least one of the co-founders at the startup pitch event who can share their observations.

Include the location, date and time, location, and host. Include notes about how you and the startup team felt the investor presentation went. Note these important points I next list.

- Did the presenter have a brain-freeze?

- Did the presenter use filler words (um, ah, like)?

- Did the presenter stutter?

- Was the presenter animated?

- Was the startup investor engaged?

- Did the presenter sound enthusiastic?

- Note the total time the presenter took to deliver the startup pitch.

- Write down any startup investor questions the presenter deferred on along with the startup investors name.

Second, you should have a bunch of business cards you collected from the Q&A session.

- Include each startup investor name, company, and Email in the Summary.

- Email each investor.

In each email, greet each startup investor by name and thank each for their attendance and great questions. If a startup investor asked a question you deferred on, include the question, and say you will send a response soon. Ask each startup investor for a follow-up 30-minute meeting (Second-Date) and suggest a couple of dates over the next five business days and with a morning or lunchtime window as possibilities.

Be sure you have the answer to any deferred question ready by the meeting.

Third, look up each startup investor on LinkedIn. Send each startup investor a connection request with a personal note about the startup investor pitch meeting.

Fourth, include each startup investors contact information from the business card into the Company contact software. Be sure to include the link to each startup investors LinkedIn page. Include in the Contact Notes section any information found on the LinkedIn page related to the college attended, and any startup worked at related to the business. The goal is to find reasons the startup investor showed interest in the market segment.

Fifth, examine the startup investors business website. Include notes to the contact software notes section about the market segments the startup investor invests and in invested companies.

Sixth, go to http://thefunded.com/ and check out the startup investors firm. Include information about positive and negative feedback about the firm itself or any partner to the contacts software notes. While you can find useful information on venture capital firms, this site does not cover individual angel or startup Seed investors well.

For angel investor research, I recommend you check out https://angel.co/. Entrepreneurs can provide reviews on angel investors on this site. Angel.co does not supply a lot of details. However, angel.co is better than no research.

Seventh, for the hosts, send each a thank you email for the opportunity to present at the startup investor event. Even if this event was part of an accelerator program you are a member of, this is a nice courtesy you should extend.

Eighth, add each startup investor to the once-a-month startup newsletter. The once-a-month startup newsletter is the perfect way to keep a warm contact warm.

This section would be incomplete unless it included a ***Do Not Do This list.***

One, avoid phone calls to the startup investor unless he or she requested a phone call. Startup investors are busy folks, and most I know to prefer email follow-ups after a startup investor pitch event.

Two, if a startup investor reaches out to you by phone, email or text, follow-up with a quick response. Any reach out from a startup investor should get a response from you within one business day. Avoid phone calls to startup investors while on a holiday or weekend. By Monday weekend emails are often forgotten. Avoid emails to startup investors after 5 pm Friday or while on the weekend. Email Monday morning after 6 am. This way the startup is fresh in the startup investors mind on Monday morning.

Three, if a startup investor asked a question which you deferred on, remember to respond with an answer promptly. Even if there is no answer ready when you send the same-day thank you email, refer to the question and set an answer-by date. Remember, if you have not received a Second-Date request from the startup investor, you can use the response to the startup investor question as an opportunity to ask for a Second-Date without being a pest.

Four, do not be a pest. If the same-day email and a second follow-up email (about a week later) does not result in a startup investor response, stop sending emails. Wait three to four weeks to send a third email. If there is no response after the third email, please stop sending emails. The likelihood of a startup investor response is near zero, and the entrepreneur continues to waste time.

Be aware that there are many reasons that startup investors do not ask for a Second-Date. You will never know for sure why any specific startup investor does not ask for a Second-Date. However, allow me to provide a few of the more common reasons for no Second-Date invitation.

One, some startup investors do not ask for a Second-Date because the startup market space is outside their sphere of interest. Even when there is no market fit for a startup investor, remember startup investors hang with other startup investors. When the startup sends all startup investors the once-a-month startup newsletter, the startup name may come up in a startup investor to startup investor conversation. Use of the startup newsletter as a follow-up is a fantastic way to discover a startup investor.

Two, some startup investors do not ask for a Second-Date because some companies are too early-stage for investment. The startup investor receipt of the once-a-month newsletter enables startup progress updates. The startup investor will reach out to the startup at an investable life-cycle stage.

Three, some startup investors do not ask for a Second-Date because the entrepreneur created a red-flag in the mind of the startup investor. Some typical red-flags are:

- The startup team was incomplete
- The Ask was unrealistic for the current revenue
- The Market Analysis was incomplete or inaccurate
- The Traction was inadequate
- The Revenue ramp was unbelievable.

If the startup survives, the team will correct inaccurate items in the startup investor pitch. The startup newsletter can refer to these changes. The startup investors receipt of the once-a-month startup newsletter, startup investors red-flags might disappear as they continue to learn about the startup.

Four, some startup investors do not ask for a Second-Date because of travel. A startup investor may have heard upwards of fifty startup pitches before they return to the office and start to do a follow-up. An entrepreneur who has written a pitch follow-up plan will know how to handle these scenarios best.

In the next chapter, I will speak about the steps left for the entrepreneur and the Investor to complete to reach — Get to the Funding Close.

Chapter Quiz

Q1: After pitch day or a first-date, take a day or two to rest and congratulate yourself on a job well done! [ ] Yes [ ] No

Q2: Immediately after the pitch, you should take all the business cards you collected and research each person. [ ] Yes [ ] No

Q3: You should wait at least a week after pitch day before emailing those potential investors you met. [ ] Yes [ ] No

Q4: Ignore the pitch day hosts. You paid them already. [ ] Yes [ ] No

Q5: You should email each potential investor every day until they respond. [ ] Yes [ ] No

Q6: Interested investors will always reach out to you. [ ] Yes [ ] No

Q7: You should ask for frank feedback from your team members on your performance. [ ] Yes [ ] No

Q8: If an investor doesn't respond to your first few emails, they are not interested, and you should quit emailing. [ ] Yes [ ] No

Q9: If an investor reaches out by phone, text, or email, you should play "hard to get" by waiting 24 hours before responding. [ ] Yes [ ] No

Q10: There was a question asked which you promised to reply to, but the truth will make things look bad, you should not respond. [ ] Yes [ ] No

Answers:

https://www.ideatogrowth.com/answers-10-slides-to-startup-funding-success/#the-first-date-pitch-follow-up

ANGEL INVESTORS TO VENTURE CAPITAL
10 SLIDES TO STARTUP FUNDING SUCCESS

Chapter Notes

_____

_____

_____

_____

_____

_____

_____

_____

_____

_____

_____

_____

_____

_____

_____

_____

_____

_____

Steps From 2nd Date to Funding Close

Figure 51 - Steps from 2nd Date thru Funding Close

You completed the first startup investor pitch (First-Date) with one or more startup investors. You have done the First-Date pitch follow-up. Now the arduous work starts to pay off. A startup investor has reached out and requested a follow-up meeting. Congratulations! You have a Second-Date invite from a startup investor.

The Second-Date — Expectations & Preparation

What is the typical startup investor focus for a Second-Date?

The Second-Date will most often be between the startup investor the entrepreneur met and the investor from the startup pitch event. However, other players may sometimes be present.

When the entrepreneur or investor sets up the Second-Date meeting, the entrepreneur needs to inquire about who will attend from the startup investors team. If the startup investor brings in a partner to the Second-Date, the entrepreneur may want to bring a co-founder. But, ask permission to do so and state the reasons as to why.

If the startup CEO is the business person and the not the technologist, both entrepreneurs should be present at all meetings with startup investors. After testing the startup CEO for a personality fit, startup investors may want to jump right into both technological and business details. The entrepreneur responsible for the technology should attend all Second-Date meetings, without exception. The same would be right for the reversed position situation.

The startup investors focus at the start of the Second-Date is to get to know the startup CEO better as a person and startup leader. Remember, most startup investors invest in people first and ideas second. Therefore, a significant investor goal of the Second-Date is to get to know the entrepreneur. The startup investor wants to determine if the startup CEO is engageable or if the startup investor will cringe at the thought of engagement with the startup CEO. No matter how good the idea, the startup investor wants to enjoy meetings with the startup CEO if the startup is investment worthy.

In many respects, the right startup investor choice is like the process of the search for a ***significant other***.

Critical entrepreneur attributes startup investors review are listed.

- Does the startup CEO have a personality fit with the Investor?
- Is the startup CEO a person of character?

- Does the startup CEO put honesty first, or find lying easy?

- Has the startup CEO been able to build a competitive team?

- Does the startup CEO refer to the team at the Second-Date?

- Is the startup CEO extroverted or introverted?

The startup investor will want to confirm any crucial points you stated about the startup. The questions can be about any of the topics you covered. You should have your laptop or tablet ready with the presentation shortcut on the home screen.

The startup investor may want to drill down on an important topic. If the startup investor has a Business background, this might be the Market plan. If the startup investor is a technologist, they may ask more focused questions around the product technology. If the startup investor has a finance background, they will ask about the Financials and Ask slides. A complete set of backup slides and a quick-jump index page on page 11 of the Investor Pitch Deck is a great way to be prepared. To address all startup investor questions with both a precise oral response and a backup slide speaks of team strength to the startup investor.

What should be the entrepreneurs focus on a Second-Date?

First, the Second-Date should be to learn more about the startup investor and the firm. Remember, if the startup investor offers to invest, and the entrepreneur accepts, both will be working together for several years. As I stated earlier, in many respects, your relationship with each startup investor shares many of the same characteristics of marriage. You are stuck with each other until the startup investor cashes out, writes off the investment in the startup, or until the board of directors fires the startup CEO. The entrepreneur needs to be sure there is a good fit between the startup investors goals, expectations, and engaging style and the startup goals and team.

Second, the entrepreneur wants to be prepared to drill down on all the crucial points covered in the startup Investor Pitch Deck. Backup slides now come into play.

So how does the entrepreneur prepare for the Second-Date?

First, do a test drive to the meeting location.

A test drive to the meeting location may seem to be a dumb thing to do. However, the knowledge of how to get to a meeting location on time is essential. Too many entrepreneurs show up late for a meeting with a startup investor. Unless you have been to the meeting location, at the same meeting time of day, how can you know you will arrive on time? Where is the nearest parking? Is the garage nearest the meeting location always full by the time of day you are meeting? How far away is the next closest garage? To show up late for a startup investor meeting is inexcusable. I urge entrepreneurs to plan to arrive 15-30 minutes early. When you plan to arrive early, you have time for some last-minute review and time to de-stress.

Second, review the backup slides and practice answers to the slides content aloud. You need to hear your responses audibly to adjust the startup Story. Practicing this way will create a dramatic difference in your delivery of the startup pitch and Q&A session.

Third, email a confirmation to the startup investor mid-afternoon of the day before the scheduled meeting confirming the time, location (address) and names of planned participants. This email acts as an essential reminder to a busy startup investor and provides the startup investor an opportunity to reschedule before surprising the entrepreneur on the day of the meeting with a cancellation or extra attendees.

Fourth, review the background of all attending startup investors via both LinkedIn and the businesses website. You will create a good impression and is a sign of respect to refer to an item in the startup investors background at the right moment.

Lastly, if the MVP is a physical product, and if the MVP is of the proper size, bring the MVP to the meeting in a box or briefcase. At the appropriate time in the conference, the entrepreneur can show the MVP to the startup investors.

Follow-up for the Second-Date will be like the follow-up to the First-Date. If the First-Date has met the startup investors' expectations, the entrepreneur will get an invite to present to the venture capital partnership - a Third-Date.

If the Second-Date meeting is with an angel investor, an expert in the market space may attend a Third-Date.

The same will often be true for many venture capital firms. Even when one of the investment partners is well versed in the market space, for more significant dollar investments, the venture capitalist will often ask the entrepreneur to meet with an expert in the market space or the technology space. I have served in this position for venture firms. A favorable outcome of the expert interview, combined with the successful completion of the due diligence checklist, often results in the entrepreneur receipt of an investment.

After the Second-Date - Partners & Expert Meetings

The entrepreneur and the lead startup investor had their Second-Date. The startup investor is still interested and wants to have the entrepreneur and the startup management team meet with some industry experts. If the startup investor is a member of a two-plus person firm, they will want the startup CEO or the startup team to meet with the partnership. I will discuss both meetings separately.

Expert Meetings

Most startup investors have a list of experts in many different fields. These fields often include the areas of technology, finance, marketing, and sales. The startup investor will also have experts in the specific field of focus of your startup they can reach out for guidance. Even when the startup investor has personal experience in the market space of the startup, experienced startup investors have learned it is wise to bring in the second set of eyes and ears to review the startup, the team, and the solution.

Partnership Pitch Meetings

Startup investors who have partners will have the entrepreneur startup pitch to the entire partnership. A successful meeting with the partnership is often the last step before the start of the Due Diligence process.

This Third-Date often occurs at the startup investor offices, most often on Monday or Friday. The entrepreneur should do the same First-Date Pitch with the same five to six-minute target. Upon completion of the startup pitch, the entire partnership will ask questions. Again, if the startup CEO is not the technical founder, the CTO should be present. The entrepreneur should ask the startup investor for guidance as to what team members they recommend you bring to the partner startup pitch meeting.

As before, the entrepreneur should keep answers short and concise. If an investment partner wants more detail than provided in the first response, they will ask a follow-up question.

Due Diligence - Should We Get Engaged?

I used the phrase Due Diligence several times throughout this book. As a reminder, the words *Due Diligence* are the magic words an entrepreneur wants to hear from a startup investor. Due Diligence means a startup investor is ready to put some significant investment effort into the evaluation of the startup.

Due diligence is a broad subject, rich in content and a topic which takes time to explain. Due Diligence is such a significant topic I decided to devote an entire book to this vital topic. See my next book titled *Due Diligence — Startup Investors Magic Words for Entrepreneurs* to learn how to achieve success in the startup investors Due Diligence process.

Convertible Notes & SAFE Notes

For any investment round in the form of a Convertible Note or SAFE Note, I want the entrepreneur to be knowledgeable before they sit down with the lawyer to draft the convertible note.

A Convertible Note is a legal document, and the entrepreneur should not grab an example from a website or a blog for immediate use. An example convertible note can be used as a draft to start the discussion with an attorney experienced in Startup Convertible Note construction. An excellent example from a reputable source may save the startup a few dollars. However, to create the Convertible Note without an attorney is an unwise decision.

Convertible Notes and SAFE - Shared Traits

Both SAFE and Convertible Notes as a viable way to help startups overcome their challenge in growing or scaling to reach critical milestones that allow a Series A round. Both SAFE and Convertible Notes can carry a discount on the next round (or current round for convertible notes).

Definition: Convertible Note

A convertible note is a debt which has the right to convert into equity upon the startup achieving an agreed upon milestone. For the layperson, you can think of a convertible note as being very similar to a regular loan. This type of loan has the option to convert into shares of preferred or common stock usually at the closing of a Series A round of financing. Some consider convertible notes to be complicated while others believe them to be simple.

Definition: SAFE

SAFE is an acronym that stands for ***Simple Agreement for Future Equity.*** It was created by the Silicon Valley accelerator <u>Y Combinator</u> as a simplify seed investment financial instrument. Similar to a convertible note, a SAFE is a warrant to purchase stock in a future priced round, usually a Series A round.

The Y-Combinator style SAFE is typically a 5-page document used most often at the Angel or Seed Round investment stage. Unlike most convertible notes, SAFE does not carry an interest rate nor a maturity date.

Equity Conversion Exit – SAFE vs. Convertible Note

SAFE and convertible notes both allow for conversion into Series A equity. A convertible note provides for the conversion into the current round of stock or a future financing event. A SAFE only provides for conversion into the next round of financing.

Convertible notes most often trigger only when a ***qualifying transaction takes place*** (more than a minimum amount dictated on the convertible note agreement) or when both the startup management team and the investors agree on the conversion.

The SAFE can convert when you raise any amount of equity investment. A SAFE does not give the entrepreneur control of when to convert, which is why the convertible note looks to be the best choice for a seed investment of this category type.

The fundraiser of common stock does not trigger conversion for a SAFE investor. If there is a need to bridge an investment round, entrepreneurs who need extra cash may have to do a *Friends and Family* investment round to avoid the conversion trigger.

Valuation Caps – SAFE vs. Convertible Note

The Entrepreneur can get a SAFE or convertible note without a valuation cap. However, it can be a challenge to pull off with either instrument. In general, the entrepreneur is advised not to set a valuation cap unless insisted on by the investor.

However, caution was raised by <u>Andrew Krowne of Dolby Family Ventures in a July 2017 article for TechCrunch:</u>

We have observed that many founders don't do the basic dilution math associated with what happens to their cap table (specifically their ownership stakes) when notes convert into equity. By avoiding setting the valuation, often multiple times, entrepreneurs often end up owning less of their startup's equity than they they thought they would. When pricing an equity round at a later point in time, entrepreneurs don't like the founder dilution numbers at all.

The bottom line is the entrepreneur must be sure they understand that even if you have a discount, by skipping the establishment of a valuation cap at the seed stage, the entrepreneur could be diluting their shares and their future investors' shares when the entrepreneur raises their Series A round.

Early Exit – SAFE vs. Convertible Note

SAFE and Convertible notes both offer similar payout mechanism in the event of a change in control (acquisition or IPO) before a conversion can occur. To participate in any buyout, the SAFE gives the investor the choice of a 1x payout or conversion into equity at the preset cap value.

A SAFE agreement can also include 2x payout provisions that are typical in a convertible debt agreement.

Interest Rate – SAFE vs. Convertible Note

SAFEs are considered to be a judicial warrant. That means a SAFE does not carry an interest rate.

Convertible Notes are considered to be a legal debt. Therefore, they carry an interest rate typically ranging from 2% to 8% (most falling around 5%).

Most entrepreneurs do not want another expense, so a SAFE would be a better choice if this were the only consideration.

Maturity Date – SAFE vs. Convertible Note

As a SAFE is considered to be a judicial warrant and not a debt instrument, a SAFE does not have a maturity date.

Convertible notes are a debt instrument and therefore have a maturity date which can cause issues when the maturity date comes to pass. Once the convertible note reaches the date of maturity, an entrepreneur has two choices:

1) Convert the debt into equity, or

2) Payback the principal plus interest

If the startup is not doing well, paying back the convertible note principal is difficult to negotiate. Inability to pay back the investors could trigger bankruptcy. Since a bankruptcy filing is not a great option for the entrepreneur, the better choice is to use a SAFE and not a convertible note.

Fees and Services – SAFE vs. Convertible Note

The entrepreneur should seek legal advice as to whether a SAFE would trigger the need for a fair (409a) valuation done by a professional services firm to formalize the valuation of the startup.

Common Terms – SAFE vs. Convertible Note

Allow me to go into a bit of detail on what some of the terms in a typical Convertible Note of SAFE.

The **Principal Amount** of a convertible note is the invested dollar amount by the noteholder. Unlike most other debt instruments, a

Convertible Note issued with an original issue discount (a price that is less than the face value of the instrument) is uncommon.

An added point is the difference between the Principal amount of each note and the Aggregate amount of the Convertible Note round. Some startup investors may prefer an aggregate cap on the amount of convertible debt a startup can fundraise in an investment round. From the startup perspective, set the aggregate cap above what you are in case you need the flexibility to fundraise. Best yet, avoid the inclusion of an aggregate cap unless startup investors insist.

The **Interest** (Rate) on a Convertible Note accrues on the investment while the note stays outstanding (i.e., until a conversion event or demand upon maturity). Interest can either be a simple rate per annum or compounded quarterly. From a startup perspective, simple interest is better as the startup team will give-up less equity down the road. For startup investors, compound interest is better because compound interest will yield a greater accrual of interest. In practice, sophisticated startup investors often avoid interest generating income investments. Therefore, the interest rate provision goes unnegotiated, and startup investors are fine with simple interest at a rate between 5% to 8%. However, higher risk often means the investor will charge a higher interest rate.

The **Maturity** date of a convertible note is the date on or after which the convertible noteholder can either demand repayment of the principal and accrued interest or trigger conversion into equity. Convertible notes in typical Seed Rounds have maturity dates of 12 to

24 months. Startups prefer more extended maturity dates as longer maturities provide the startup more time to close the next investment round. Longer maturities also will delay the noteholders ability to demand repayment of the note or trigger a conversion on the maturity date.

A **Discount** (Rate) is a method of compensation enhancement used by startups to compensate Seed Investment Round startup investors for the higher risk taken versus startup investors who come in at a later round. Convertible Notes offer noteholders the benefit of conversion into preferred equity at a discount to the price paid by the later startup investors at a qualified financial event. The standard discount offered to convertible noteholders in a Seed Investment Round is often 20% to 25%. A discount rate of 20% means if the price per share paid by the future new startup investors at a later Qualified Financial event is USD 100 per share, then the convertible noteholders would receive the same shares at a discounted price of USD 80 per share (USD 100 minus the 20% discount). One calculates the number of shares a convertible noteholder would receive by the addition of the principal amount of the note plus accrued interest and divides the sum by the discounted price per share.

The Ask Slide lacks some topics the entrepreneur should be ready to answer with one of the backup slides.

- Conversion Triggers
- Qualified Financial Conversion
- Corporate Transaction Conversion

- Maturity Conversion
- Valuation Cap

A **Qualified Financial Conversion** occurs when the startup does a qualified financial round (i.e., a Series A round). Conversion is what both the startup and the convertible noteholders want to have happened. When such a conversion occurs, the principal amount, plus accrued interest, convert into preferred stock is the same as what the new startup investors at the qualified financial event (i.e., a Series A round) receive.

In some cases, Convertible Notes can convert into Shadow Preferred Stock. With this type of stock limits the liquidation preference to the noteholders investment. The value of the preferred stock acquired at a discount upon conversion avoids consideration. The valuation cap or discount rate determines the amount of preferred stock the convertible noteholder receives.

A **Corporate Transaction Conversion** happens if the startup sells or merges with another startup before a Qualified Financial Conversion. If either occurs, then convertible noteholders can elect to (a) Convert into common stock to share in the proceeds of a sale of the startup alongside the other common shareholders (i.e., the founders) or (b) Repayment of the principal amount plus accrued interest.

Most often, noteholders will choose whichever option results in a more significant cash payment. In some cases, Convertible Notes provide for a corporate transaction premium. The transaction premium is often a multiple of the principal amount of the convertible note the noteholder is entitled to receive. For example, if a Convertible Note has a 2x Corporate Transaction Premium, then the noteholder should receive accrued interest on the original principal amount, plus two times the principal amount of the note.

A **Maturity Conversion** can occur at any time on or after the Maturity date stated on the Convertible Note. Startup investors in Convertible Notes often seek to share in the equity upside of a startup and repayment with interest is of little importance. It is rare for Convertible Noteholders to demand repayment at the maturity of the note. Chances are high the startup will lack the liquid capital to repay the convertible notes anyway. A note repayment demand by a noteholder would result in the loss of all or part of the investment. The note holder would lose the opportunity to share in future equity upside. Instead, noteholders often agree to extend maturity or elect to convert into common stock.

Should I Choose a Convertible Note or a SAFE?

Each startup CEO and their team must make this decision. I cannot make this decision for you. I have out outlined the commonalities and the differences for you to be able to make the best choice for yourself.

Part of this decision will also come from each investor you engage. Some will prefer convertible notes. Some will prefer a SAFE. Some will not be familiar with a SAFE and will have to take time to research. Some will not agree to either a convertible note or a SAFE and insist on a purchase of preferred or common stock.

Remember to consult an attorney who has substantial experience with Startup Convertible Notes and SAFEs when you construct your investment round legal documents.

Term Sheet - Proposal of Marriage

Due Diligence is complete. It is time for either the startup CEO or the investor to present a term sheet.

What? As the startup CEO, you are telling me that I can present a term sheet to the investor?

Yes!

Just like it is becoming more common for a girl to propose marriage to a boy, the entrepreneur can suggest the terms of marriage to the investor.

ANGEL INVESTORS TO VENTURE CAPITAL
10 SLIDES TO STARTUP FUNDING SUCCESS

In most contract negotiations it is well known that the first party to present the written contract (almost) always ends up with the final agreement being more in their favor.

The startup CEO presenting the term sheet also tends to move the investment round to a quicker close. When the entrepreneur has spent the time and legal monies to draft the term sheet and present it first, the investor wastes less to think about terms and crafting their own.

In many investment rounds, the startup is going to have more than one investor, so the startup is creating and presenting the term sheet to all investors is more time efficient. Once one of the multiple investors has agreed to the startup's term sheet, the startup can push back against any other investor requesting changes.

What is a Term Sheet?

A term sheet is a non-binding agreement between a startup founder and the startup investor(s). It covers funding terms, employee option pools, and governance. Term sheets can be full of legal language and be a challenge to understand, especially for first-time founders.

Term sheets can be *founder friendly* or not *founder friendly*. Founder Friendly is a phrase that does what it says. The term sheet wording defers all contractual terms in favor of the founder over the investor.

Term sheets can be one page, but most will be several pages. There are crucial issues that must be in the term sheet.

- Company name issuing the note or stock

- Type of collateral (Convertible Note, SAFE or Stock)
- The valuation
- Offering Amount
- If the sale of shares: Shares and price
- What happens on liquidation or IPO
- Voting rights
- Board seats
- Conversion options
- Anti-dilution provisions
- Investors rights to information
- Founders obligations
- Who pays legal expenses
- Non-disclosure requirements
- Rights to future investment
- Signatures

What is also crucial in a founder-friendly term sheet is what is NOT in the term sheet.

- The startup does not pay investors legal fees.

Requiring the startup to pay the investor(s) legal fees is outrageous. The startup can make better use of the investor's money.

- No Employee Stock Option Pool

Taking the option pool out of the pre-money valuation (i.e., diluting only founders and not investors for future hires) is just a way to manipulate the startup's valuation artificially. New hires benefit both the startup and the investors so new employees should dilute everyone.

- No Investment Offer Expiration Date

Sometimes an investor created term sheet will include a five to ten-day expiration. An investment offer with a short expiration is the investors attempt to force the startup management into a quick decision in favor of that investor.

In practice, startup management teams make a quick decision.

If the startup is the first to place a term sheet rather than the investor do you need an expiration date? No. If you have multiple investors each of whom have completed due diligence and wanted to invest, the term sheet wording can state that the round closes when all the investment dollars are spoken for by investors signing and returning the term sheet.

Be careful if you do send out a term sheet to multiple investors simultaneously. If two or more investors want to take the entire round, the startup team should first decide who they prefer to work with and send that investor the term sheet. If that investor balks at many of the terms and suggests terms that are not founder friendly, then I suggest you send the term sheet to the second investor. If the second investor agrees to all or most of the terms and signs, then the first investor has self-selected out of the investment opportunity in your startup. You should call and thank them for their interest and inform them that another investor has agreed to fund this investment round.

2nd DATE THRU FUNDING CLOSE

If this round requires multiple investors to raise the full amount of the fund-raiser, send all interested parties the startup created term sheet at the same time. After one business day, check with each investor by phone and ask if they have any questions. Take note of any concerns they have but do not commit to changes. Once you have feedback from all interested investors who have reviewed the term sheet, send out a revised term sheet for review. The revised term sheet does not need to include all changes from all investors. However, if there was a 100% shared set of requested modifications, and those changes are acceptable to the startup team, include them in the revised term sheet.

If a few of the investors refuse to sign the revised term sheet, the startup team has a few options.

One, ask the investors who agree with the revised term sheet to make a more substantial investment

Two, seek additional investors willing to conform to the revised term sheet

Three, make further term sheet changes to get enough investors to close the investment round

- No confidentiality.

Founder and investor relationships are long-lasting. Founders should talk to whomever they want, and if they are going to tell people what the investor offered them, they should be free to do so. From experience, I can tell you that Investors share with each other what they offer companies.

- No participating preferred, non-standard liquidation preference, etc.

There should be a 1x liquidation preference, but some investors are willing to forgo a 1x liquidation and buy common shares. However, this can have implications for the strike price for employee options, so most founders do not want it.

Several outfits have published excellent articles and term sheet examples that I will refer you to. You can find two of the better ones at:

Forward Partners - https://www.businessinsider.com/foward-partners-pre-seed-startup-term-sheet-public-2018-1

Sam Altman - http://blog.samaltman.com/a-founder-friendly-term-sheet

The Close of the Investment Round — All Say — *I Do*

If you have not done so already, find a startup-savvy lawyer. The most efficient closing processes I have experienced were when the startup has a reputable attorney who regularly represents startups.

I would also encourage the startup CEO to ask your lawyer to explain the *Why* behind their recommended steps.

I am not a lawyer, so I am only going to address the closing process which takes place *after* the startup CEO has finalized the term sheet and you have drafted the final investment documents.

A great closing process minimizes the following procedures:

- The number of hours investors spend filling out the documents and delivering the funds

- The number of days between when investors verbally commit to the time when they fund

- The number of times the entrepreneur requests information from investors

- The total legal fees

- The number of hours the entrepreneur spends seeking information from investors

- The number of hours the entrepreneur spends filling out paperwork

Ask your lawyer and your accountant to give you a list of all the things they will need from your investors throughout the total time of the investment. The list will likely include:

- Mailing addresses of each investor

- Investor accreditation verification signed the form

- Criminal Background Checks (this may only be a requirement from certain investors)

- Social security or tax ID numbers [for K-1s used for convertible notes]

I would recommend collecting any information you will need in the future with any documentation you will need to finalize the initial investment. Doing so will minimize the time you will spend tracking it down later.

Once you have your information list, work with your lawyer to create an electronic folder includeing the following information to use for the closing signature packet:

- The signed term sheets

- Investor instructions on how to fill out and return the investment documents and fund the investment

- The payment instructions should include wire instructions. Investors typically wire their funds, but I would also include instructions to pay by check.

- All the signature pages for each document your investors need to sign [You will need the finalized investment documents for this]. It is customary for investors to sign and return only the signature pages. If you use DocuSign, I will insert signature fields directly on the signature page within each document. I would suggest creating a signature packet since some investors may prefer not to use DocuSign.

2nd DATE THRU FUNDING CLOSE

Next, you want to figure out how and when to send these documents. To determine this, you will need to determine a couple of things:

- Do you need to close every investor at once?

Many lawyers and investors encourage entrepreneurs to gather signatures and accept funds all at once on a specified closing date. This approach is rarely necessary. If your lawyer or lead investor suggests this, question his/her logic before agreeing. It is much easier to close investors as soon as they commit.

- Is there a minimum close requirement?

Often yes. Some investors want to be sure that sufficient money has been raised to support the company growth plan before committing their funds. I would recommend meeting somewhere in the middle and proposing a dollar amount that will at least support conservative growth. Between 30% and 50% of the total of the entire round, is a fair amount to allow a first close, followed by a rolling investment close.

After determining the above two items:

- Get investors verbal commitments to investing

When you meet with prospective investors, get as much buy-in as possible before sending the documents for review and signature. Discuss the details of the deal and the how much they plan to invest.

- Send all documents that are ready for signature:

As soon as investors verbally commit, send on any materials they can sign to firm up their commitment. For example:

- If you have final documents, but you have not yet hit your minimum close requirement, send investors the final documents to sign and return. Send wire instructions as soon as you collect enough signatures to hit a minimum close to prevent investors from wiring funds too early.

- Once you have final documents and have hit the minimum close requirement, send final documents and wire instructions and close the deal.

- Upon receipt of signed documents and the wire or check clears, send countersigned documents. Set up alerts on your company bank account, so you receive an email each time a wire posts.

Next are a few general tips:

- Do not send paper documents (unless asked). It is a waste of paper and annoys many investors.

- Send electronic documents in pdf format.

- All legal documents you send should be in pdf format. Use DocuSign for all investors, if possible.

- Use Track Changes (or similar) to redline docs for changes.

- Tell your lawyer to optimize the documents for DocuSign.

- Insert signature fields directly on the signature page within each document rather than attaching a signature packet.

Chapter Quiz

Q1: On a second-date, the Entrepreneur should ask the interested investor who from the Entrepreneurs team should attend and who from investors side will attend? [ ] Yes [ ] No

Q2: You've never been to the location of the second-date. What should you do prior to the meeting date?

Q3: You should confirm the meeting date, time, and location one business day prior with them or their admin. [ ] Yes [ ] No

Q4: You should spend no more than 10% of the meeting time asking questions of the investor. [ ] Yes [ ] No

Q5: The second-date is about both sides determining if there is enough mutual interest to justify a third-date. [ ] Yes [ ] No

Q6: Both a Convertible Note and a SAFE allow for conversion into stock at the current round price and terms. [ ] Yes [ ] No

Q7: A Valuation Cap always helps the Entrepreneur. [ ] Yes [ ] No

Q8: Doing a closing round is easy and you should skip using a CPA and lawyer to save big dollars! [ ] Yes [ ] No

Q9: You must close all investors on the same day. [ ] Yes [ ] No

Q10: The Entrepreneur's company should pay all investor legal costs. [ ] Yes [ ] No

Answers:

https://www.ideatogrowth.com/answers-10-slides-to-startup-funding-success/#2nd-date-thru-funding-close

Chapter Notes

_____

_____

_____

_____

_____

_____

_____

_____

_____

_____

_____

_____

_____

_____

_____

_____

_____

_____

_____

Figure 52 - The Q&A

The Entrepreneurs Frequently Asked Questions chapter was one of the harder sections to write. The creation of a list of frequent questions that entrepreneurs ask about how to raise fund-raise was more of a challenge than I expected.

To create the Q&A chapter was a challenge as to what to exclude from the list. As you might imagine, I covered a lot of questions in the content of the book. However, to include every topic item is impossible. I wanted to keep the book at under 200 pages in 6-inch x 9-inch format as few entrepreneurs have the time to read a wordy book. In this light, here are some of the most frequent questions.

Q1: Does the startup need revenue to fundraise?

A1: No. But with conditions. My teams have fundraised upwards of more than USD 100M across the span of several companies without a single dollar of revenue. The tradeoff was a lot of ownership went to the startup investors when did a pre-revenue fundraise. Therefore, I recommend the entrepreneur to avoid a fundraiser until the avoidance of fundraising is too painful.

Q2: Do I have to have two other co-founders to fundraise?

A2: No. But again, with conditions. Solopreneurs, the nickname of entrepreneurial teams of one, face a much bigger uphill battle with a fundraiser than startup teams of three or more people.

I do not invest in Solopreneur startups. If I find a great Solopreneur who needs a team, I am happy to work with the entrepreneur while they bring together a three-person team. When the startup team is complete, I will often invest.

Some venture firms take the same approach not to miss great solopreneurs who have a great idea but still need a team.

Q3: Do I have to have a Minimum Viable Product (MVP) to fundraise?

A3: No. But again, with conditions. My teams and I have fundraised more than USD 100M across the span of several companies without an MVP. Many other companies do the same.

However, in our case, there was a seasoned, proven team with a great idea and an immense and rapid growing target market. However, a lot of ownership of the startup ended up with the startup investors, which is why I recommend the avoidance of a pre-MVP fundraises.

Q4: If I do not need OPM to grow my startup, is there any reason I should seek startup investors?

A4: Yes. I meet several entrepreneurs each year who have bootstrapped companies to profitability. These entrepreneurs take all the positive cash flow and feed the free cash flow back into the growth of the startup. The problem is most often the entrepreneur is neither paying themselves or the startup team market salaries and benefits. While many founders and co-founders recognize low to no wages are often a reality early in the life of a startup, to do so for more than a year or two is often both a financial and mental burden. The choice to use OPM funds to grow the startup will cost you some of the ownership. However, done correctly, the use of OPM will often enable the startup to grow faster, and gain more in value sooner, than the startup ownership you sold. Bootstrapping the startup is an excellent idea, up to a point. Take the investment capital at the right time, and the right price and the startup are both bigger and happier.

Q5: Should I join an Accelerator even if my startup generates more than USD 10K MRR?

A5: Yes, if the Accelerator has a support organization. Few Accelerators have post accelerator program support. The Tampa Bay WaVE (www.tampabaywave.org) is one example of a high-technology accelerator with long-term entrepreneurial support.

In (2018) if you are a high-technology startup, for the low membership fee of USD 200/month you get access to 100+ Mentors who have real-world work experience in every field of expertise you can imagine.

You also become part of the Union Platform (www.union.vc) to access Mentors around the world. As a Union platform member, you get access to vendor discounts worth many tens of thousands of dollars (USD).

Q6: My search for funds while in the last six months has been unsuccessful. What should I do?

A6: First, know this is normal. Most first-time entrepreneurs take a long time to fundraise. The first step is for the entrepreneur is to implement most of the teachings in this book.

Next, you should search for the local One Million Cups (www.1millioncups.com) to startup pitch the latest startup pitch deck. After you give your startup investor startup pitch, ask the startup investor for frank and honest feedback. Listen to the startup investor feedback and take corrective actions.

Consider the fundraising of a smaller investment round or continue to bootstrap the startup until the startup reaches a significant milestone. Often the startup progress is insufficient for the startup investors to invest. The more you can de-risk the startup, the easier it will be to fundraise.

Hire a Business Coach with experience and work with entrepreneurs. In one hour, you can get some great feedback on what the next steps should be. Implement good suggestions and attempt a fundraiser for another six months.

If you are still struggling after another six months to get First-Dates or Second-Dates, then the idea or the team is too weak to get a fundraiser. It may be time to return to the drawing board and search for the next great idea to pursue. Do not feel bad if you must move onto another idea and team. Most serial entrepreneurs have false starts. I know because I am one as are most of the serial entrepreneurs I know.

Q7: My family members have offered to invest in my startup. Should I allow this investment?

A7: Maybe. My grandparents taught me that you are stuck with your family for life. However, you can change the people you work with on any day you feel the need. I caution entrepreneurs against the use of family funds in the first stages of a business as the risk of failure is extremely high. Even if the amount of capital allowed to invest is less than 5% of net worth if the startup fails and the Friends and Family lose all the investment, this loss will haunt them, and the entrepreneur, forever.

Once the startup has significant revenue and profits, the entrepreneur can always have a small Friends and Family investment round to allow ownership of a piece of the business. Friends and Family will still get the pride and bragging rights of an investment in the company, without the enormous risk involved.

Insist (in writing) on the disclosure of each startup investor net worth. Limit each Friend and Family investment to a maximum of 5% of net worth. 2% to 3% is even better. If at some point the Friends and Family investment is wiped-out, the entrepreneur has minimized the harm to each Friend and Family members long-term financial wealth. This discussion alone should indicate the enormous risk to each Friend and Family member. Each Friend and Family member should review any investment in the startup as a risk no better than the choice of red or black at the roulette table. If any Friends and Family member is uncomfortable with this analogy, refuse an early stage investment from this Friends and Family member.

Q8: I have received a Term Sheet from a startup investor. I am unfamiliar with all the terms and conditions. What should I do?

A8: First steps first. Congratulations. You have a *Fish (Investor) on the Hook.*

The correct next step is to call the startup lawyer who reviewed or created the incorporation documents and shareholder agreements. Schedule an hour to discuss the term sheet.

A good lawyer will explain all the terms and educate you on any counteroffers you should consider if any conditions are unfavorable to the startup. Now is the time to spend dollars and use your startup lawyer.

Q9: My co-founder and I are in constant disagreement and to move forward as a team is impossible. What should I do?

A9: A constant conflict between co-founders, is untenable for the long term. Startup investors will often sniff out disputes between co-founders quickly. Unresolved conflicts could result in startup investors avoiding investment in the startup.

If the entrepreneur has created the proper shareholder and founder agreements, this documentation will describe what happens when the CEO determines the continued employment of the co-founder is unfavorable to the Company. The startup lawyer should explain the situation and guide the CEO through the co-founder termination process. Often the startup lawyer will bring in a lawyer who specializes in HR issues to handle the process.

If you skimped on legal review and lacked the legal documents which specify the termination process, the lawyer will outline what the options are to terminate a co-founder. I can tell you I have seen the termination process of a co-founder destroys a startup.

However, if the relationship has turned toxic and the problem co-founder, does not volunteer to leave, to close the startup may be the final choice. A new startup can start with the rest of the team and without the problem co-founder. While the termination of a co-founder may be painful in the short-term, the startup should be back on track often within six months or less. This time pay the lawyers up front and have robust founder agreement termination clauses.

In the next chapter, I will speak about wrapping up this book and my teachings — The Epilogue.

Also, be sure to check out the Resources page for helpful downloads! There is also a link to save you dozens of hours building your own Investor Pitch Deck Slide template. For book buyers I include a discount code that will save you $$$.

Click RESOURCES to jump to the download page now.

Great Teams & Good Ideas Raise Investment Capital.

Figure 53 - Epilogue - Great Teams + Good Ideas Raise Investment Capital

My experience is that great teams and good ideas will (usually) successfully fundraise. It is sad when they are unable to fund-raise, but the reasons for failure are often avoidable.

However, since startup investors often will not inform the entrepreneur why there is no Second-Date, Third-Date, or why startup investors never say **We want to begin Due Diligence**, the startup is unable to take any corrective action. Often the startup dies before the startup gets off the ground.

I want to help you avoid this result.

I was fortunate to spend more than 25 years in the Silicon Valley startup world. I experienced both successes and failures. As I write this book, I have moved back to my home state of Florida three years plus ago, and now live in Tampa Florida. The Tampa Bay area has a vibrant High Technology entrepreneurial spirit, and I continue to help startups find good footing and grow into successful companies in whatever way I can see to help.

Billionaires like Jeff Vinik and Bill Gates have already committed billions of dollars to rebuild swathes of the downtown bayfront with millions of square feet of new buildings targeted to small, medium and million square foot corporate headquarters.

In addition to the Tampa Bay WaVE Accelerator and St. Petersburg TEC Garage, Jeff Vinik as already founded an Innovation Hub as part of the new office space is under construction (2018). Together, these organizations will ensure continued entrepreneurs in the Tampa Bay region.

I strive to do my small part here and also achieve my give-back with the authorship of this book. With this book, its companion courses, guides, blog posts, plus several planned to follow-on books I am passing on my experience in starting and running companies and in how to raise investment funds.

I want to share my hard-earned experience of the things I have seen that work and those I have observed that do not work so your startup has the highest likelihood of success.

If I can help you avoid even one of the many landmines the entrepreneur finds in their path, I have achieved my goal of sharing what I learned from both my experience and from the learnings from several Mentors who helped me throughout my career.

I hope you will learn from my teachings in this book. I do not expect the entrepreneur to follow 100% of what I teach herein. An essential part of the entrepreneur's journey is the discovery of your unique path to success. I hope this book will help you choose the best route to turn your idea into a high growth company.

In the end, the entrepreneur's success or failure is 100% up to the entrepreneur, the team, the product, the startup investors and the customers. I hope that both the startup entrepreneur and the startup investors learn from this book will help guide you to the best possible outcome in the discovery of the capital needed to grow a successful company and the startups that can multiply the investor's investment.

In the next chapter, I will take a moment to speak a bit about myself, so you will know a bit more about Kenneth Ervin Young and why I wrote this book

Also, be sure to check out the Resources page for helpful downloads! There is also a link to save you dozens of hours building your own Investor Pitch Deck Slide template. For book buyers I include a discount code that will save you $$$.

Click <u>RESOURCES</u> to jump to the download page now.

ABOUT THE AUTHOR

Figure 54 - Kenneth Ervin Young

Kenneth is a serial entrepreneur (1 IPO + 2 M&A), Founder & CEO of IDEA TO GROWTH LLC. Kenneth helps others through his activities as a Startup & Executive Coach and Software Developer. Kenneth also gives back as a Mentor and Investor Pitch Coach at the Tampa Bay WaVE High Technology Startup Accelerator.

Kenneth spent 32 years in Silicon Valley where he co-founded several high technology companies. He has a bachelor's in electrical engineering (BEE) from the Georgia Institute of Technology.

Kenneth moved to Tampa FL in June 2015 to return to his state of birth and to assist the Tampa Bay High Technology Entrepreneurial movement to accelerate towards becoming the High Technology Hub of the South.

I enjoy helping other High-Technology entrepreneurs through the Idea-Build-Launch-Growth Business Phase. I was fortunate to have a few great Mentors help me with guidance at critical points in my career. I look to give back by helping other entrepreneurs.

Kenneth's current startup, IDEA TO GROWTH LLC (https://www.IdeaToGrowth.com), offers Executive Coaching, Website Development & Software-as-a-Service (SaaS) products to companies ranging in size from the startup BUILD Stage all the way through the corporate GROWTH Stage.

For more information, contact:

Kenneth Ervin Young

CEO & Founder

IDEA TO GROWTH LLC

ken@IdeaToGrowth.com

www.IdeaToGrowth.com

www.twitter.com/IdeaToGrowth

www.linkedin.com/in/KennethErvinYoung

https://www.facebook.com/IdeaToGrowth

https://www.LinkedIn.com/company/Idea-To-Growth-LLC/

REFERENCES

- USA National organization targeted to help local startup entrepreneurs. Click this link to find out more

  https://www.1millioncups.com/

- A great organization where you want frank feedback on your speaking skills, more than the startup pitch content, I recommend you join Toast Masters

  (https://www.toastmasters.org)

- Forward   Partners   -

  https://www.businessinsider.com/foward-partners-pre-seed-startup-term-sheet-public-2018-1

- Sam Altman - http://blog.samaltman.com/a-founder-friendly-term-sheet

THIS PAGE INTENTIONALLY LEFT BLANK

RESOURCES

- Register as a Book Owner and Get Your FREE Downloads - https://www.ideatogrowth.com/contact-book-owner-10-slides-to-startup-funding-success/

- **100% FREE** Startup Business Life-Cycle Checklist. https://www.ideatogrowth.com/contact-free-download-startup-business-life-cycle-checklist/

- Due Diligence Coaching Course and SaaS Product, and my book buyers get a jump to the front of my early adopter list. https://www.ideatogrowth.com/contact-book-waitlist-investor-due-diligence-book/

- To aid you in your decision in whether the time is right for you to take OPM, I have made a **100% FREE** OPM Checklist you can download from my website link I share next: https://www.ideatogrowth.com/contact-free-download-opm-checklist/

- Buy a tripod onto which you can mount your phone. Record every practice. Here is one on Amazon which works well, is portable and works with most any phone: https://www.amazon.com/DIGIANT-Aluminum-Universal-Smartphone-Smartphones/dp/B018ICYNKY/

- Here you will find a link for a FREE copy to my Investor Pitch Deck Verbal Practice Checklist: https://ideatogrowth.com/contact-free-download-investor-pitch-deck-verbal-practice-checklist/

ANGEL INVESTORS TO VENTURE CAPITAL
10 SLIDES TO STARTUP FUNDING SUCCESS

- Download the Complete Investor Pitch Deck Checklist - **100% FREE**:

  https://www.ideatogrowth.com/contact-free-download-investor-pitch-deck-checklist

- Get the Investor Pitch Deck Slide Templates – **Use the below link to SAVE BIG $$$!**:

  https://www.ideatogrowth.com/coupon-10-slides-to-startup-funding-success/#pitch-deck-slide-50%-discount-coupon

Made in the USA
Coppell, TX
02 September 2021